The QC Problem-Solving Approach

The QC Problem-Solving Approach

Solving Workplace Problems
the Japanese Way

KATSUYA HOSOTANI

JUSE Press

Tokyo, Japan

Originally published in Japan as *QC-teki Mondai Kaiketsuhō* (The QC Problem-Solving Approach) by Katsuya Hosotani, published by JUSE Press, Ltd. ©Katsuya Hosotani 1989.

The QC Problem-Solving Approach
Solving Workplace Problems
the Japanese Way

First Edition······January 2018

Published by JUSE Press, Ltd.
5-15-5 Sendagaya, Shibuya-ku, Tokyo 151-0051, Japan
URL http://www.juse-p.co.jp/

All rights reserved. No part of this book may be reproduced in any form or by any means, without permission in writing from the publisher.

Translated by J. H. Loftus

First English Edition published by 3A Corporation(1992)

ISBN978-4-8171-9638-5 C0034
Printed in Japan

Preface

The business environment enveloping companies both at home and abroad is becoming harsher and harsher. To ensure their continuance in our rapidly changing industrial society, corporations are adopting various survival strategies under the "Quality First" banner. These strategies include actively pursuing technical innovation, instituting sweeping organizational reforms, and stripping away unprofitable divisions.

Meanwhile, our workplaces are also undergoing tremendous upheavals: CIM (Computer Integrated Manufacturing) and OA (Office Automation) are being introduced, and production lines are constantly being reorganized and rearranged. The roles of department managers, foremen, group leaders, team leaders, chief clerks, charge hands, supervisors, and others in managerial and supervisory positions are becoming more and more important. There has never been a greater need for competent workplace leaders.

But what are competent workplace leaders? I believe they are people able to formulate and solve problems.

In a sense, life is a continual problem-solving process. From birth to death, we keep running into difficulties. Of course, we could go through life avoiding problems or pretending they did not exist, but this would be a life of escapism. To live our brief lives fully, we must be ready, willing, and able to solve problems effectively.

In turbulent times like today's, we must constantly discover, formulate, and solve serious new problems. If we do not, we will not fulfill our roles as workplace leaders and our companies will not realize their full potential. We will then fail to create true purpose in the lives of our employees and co-workers.

I do not think that problem-solving ability is possessed only by certain types of people or that it is an inborn faculty. Rather, it is something that

v

develops with experience and can be cultivated through repeated theoretical study and hands-on practice.

The QC (Quality Control) problem-solving approach is being used with great success in all areas of Total Quality Management. This book explains the following main aspects of the approach simply and clearly, tying them in to actual practice as far as possible:

1. The meaning and significance of the QC problem-solving approach.
2. The QC viewpoint needed for the QC problem-solving approach.
3. Putting the QC problem-solving approach into practice.
4. Using QC tools as part of the QC problem-solving approach.

The aim of this book is to enable readers to master the QC problem-solving approach by studying how to formulate problems, learning about the QC viewpoint, the QC Seven-Step Problem-Solving Formula and the QC tools, and discovering how to put these into practice.

I will be more than happy if the book can help to develop the new type of "problem-solving workplace leaders" that we will need in the future and create cheerful, purposeful workplaces with problem-solving muscle.

The completion of this book was due in large measure to the instruction and advice I have received over the years from my teachers and mentors in the QC world, to whom I am deeply grateful. I should also like to express my gratitude to all concerned for their kind permission to use the case studies presented here.

Finally, I should like to thank all the people at JUSE Press who helped so much with the publication of this book, especially Katsuharu Arai (Director, President's Office), Kohei Yokota (Director, Sales Department), Hikoyasu Shimizu (Section Manager, Editorial Department), and Takafumi Toba (Editorial Department).

KATSUYA HOSOTANI

October 1989

Kinki QC Circle Chapter 25th Anniversary Convention
Suita City Cultural Hall

How to Use This Book

This book is intended to serve as a practical manual for solving problems in the workplace. Solving problems in the areas of quality (Q), cost (C), delivery (D), safety (S), and morale (M) is the essence of Total Quality Management.

The "QC problem-solving approach" means solving problems rationally, scientifically, efficiently, and effectively using three powerful features: the QC viewpoint, the Seven-Step QC Problem-Solving Formula, and the QC tools.

I hope readers will make use of this book to master the QC problem-solving approach, either through in-house group training or by individual self-study. It is planned to publish a sequel, provisionally titled "QC Problem-Solving exercises," shortly. Since this will consist mainly of a collection of case studies corresponding to the material in the present book, I urge readers to make use of it also.

Who Is This Book For?

Although this book is intended chiefly for front-line workplace supervisors, I have also tried to make it useful for people at a wide range of levels. In terms of the company organization, this means everyone from ordinary employees and supervisors through support staff to department and division managers. In QC circle terms, it means everyone from circle members through circle leaders to facilitators.

viii   HOW TO USE THIS BOOK

How Should the Book Be Used?

This book can be used, among other ways, as follows:

1. As the principal textbook for in-house QC problem-solving seminars. The table below shows a typical timetable for an in-house seminar based on the book.
2. As a regular QC seminar textbook or reference book.
3. As a manual for use when tackling problems or when problem-solving activities have become bogged down.

Example of Timetable for In-Company Seminar Based on This Book

Time	Title of Lecture	Chapter
9:00–9:20	The Importance of Problem-Solving	1
9:20–9:40	The Meaning and Significance of the QC Problem-Solving Approach	2
9:40–10:50	The QC Viewpoint Needed for the QC Problem-Solving Approach	3
11:00–12:00	Putting the QC Problem-Solving Approach into Practice	4
13:00–14:00	Using QC Tools as Part of the QC Problem-Solving Approach	5
14:10–14:50	Presentation and Examination of QC Problem-Solving Case Studies	6
14:50–16:30	Group Discussion—"Learning from Problem-Solving Case Studies"	All
16:30–17:00	Presentation and Evaluation of Group Discussion Conclusions	All

Note: (1) Whenever possible, select examples from your own company as problem-solving case studies; (2) in group discussions, evaluate and report on case studies in terms of "good points" (with reasons), "points requiring improvement" (with reasons), and "details of improvements."

How Should the Book Be Read?

This book can be read in the following ways:

1. In order, from beginning to end, starting with Chapter 1. This method is preferable when possible.
2. By starting with the chapter that interests you most.

HOW TO USE THIS BOOK

3. By using the table of contents or index to locate the appropriate place when you meet a problem, and reading the parts you need.

How Should the Book Be Studied?

The book can be used as a study aid in the following ways:

1. Hold in-company seminars using the book as the main text. If possible, invite an outside QC expert as lecturer. When this is impossible, use an experienced person from within the company.
2. Form training or study groups to read the book aloud in turns and discuss it.
3. Use the book for self-study.

I have mentioned various ways of reading and studying this book, but the most important thing is to practice what you learn. This is bound to increase your experience and raise your own personal problem-solving ability.

About the Author

KATSUYA HOSOTANI was born in 1938, graduated from the Faculty of Engineering of the Osaka Institute of Technology in 1960, and received a consulting engineer in Management Engineering in 1968. He retired from his post as Senior Assistant to Director to Kinki Telecommunications Bureau of Nippon Telegraph and Telephone Public Corporation (NTT) in 1983, and is now Director of the QC Research Institute, a JUSE Consultant, and Adviser to the Japanese Standards Association. Mr. Hosotani has a lifetime of experience in QC and has written and co-authored many instructional books.

Contents

Preface   v

How to Use This Book   vii

About the Author   xi

Chapter 1 The Importance of Problem Solving   1

    1.1 The Role of Workplace Leaders   1
        Competent workplace leaders now required
    1.2 Good Problem Solvers   5
        Which type are you?
    1.3 What Is a Strong Workplace?   7
        Tackling more challenging problems
    1.4 Problem Solving and TQC   8
        Promoting firmly grounded TQC activities

**Chapter 2 What Is the QC Problem-Solving
          Approach?   13**

    2.1 What Is a Problem?   13
        Narrowing the gap between the ideal and the real
        2.1.1   The Definition of a Problem   13
        2.1.2   Classifying Problems   14
    **2.2 A Definition of the QC Problem-Solving
          Approach   17**
        Use the QC approach to crack your problems
        2.2.1   Problem-Solving Methods   17

2.2.2 The QC Problem-Solving Approach and Its
Benefits   17

**2.3 The Ten Commandments for Becoming a Competent
Problem Solver   19**
Some tips for becoming good problem-solving leaders

Chapter 3 The QC Viewpoint—Vital for QC-Type Problem Solving   21

3.1 The QC Mindset   21
The QC viewpoint is vital
3.2 "Quality First"   23
Above all, produce good quality
3.2.1 What Is "Quality First"?   23
3.2.2 Case Study: Preventing Careless Mistakes by
Error-Proofing   25
3.3 Consumer Orientation   26
Make the products the customer really wants
3.3.1 What Is Consumer Orientation?   26
3.3.2 Case Study: Consumer Orientation in Hospital
Reception Work   28
3.4 The Next Process Is Your Customer   33
*Never send defectives or mistakes on to the next
process*
3.4.1 What Does "The Next Process Is Your
Customer" Mean?   33
3.4.2 Case Study: Providing Tools that Satisfy the
Next Process   34
3.5 The PDCA Wheel   37
Rotate the PDCA wheel diligently
3.5.1 What Is Management?   37
3.5.2 Case Study: PDCA on a Construction
Site   41
3.6 Priority Consciousness   43
*Pounce on priority problems and attack them
mercilessly*
3.6.1 What Is Priority Consciousness?   43
3.6.2 Case Study: Priority Consciousness in
Education and Dissemination   43
3.7 Management by Fact   48
Speak with facts and data

CONTENTS   xv

3.7.1 What Is Management by Fact?   48
3.7.2 Case Study: Reconstructing Defect Generation
       Mechanism by VTR   50
3.8 Process Control   51
Control working methods, not results
3.8.1 What Is Process Control?   51
3.8.2 Case Study: Process-Oriented Sales in Order
       Management   53
3.9 Dispersion Control   55
Pay attention to dispersion and identify its causes
3.9.1 What Is Dispersion Control?   55
3.9.2 Case Study: Controlling Pile Installation
       Precision in Subway Construction   56
3.10 Recurrence Prevention   59
*Institute radical countermeasures to ensure that the
same mistake is not repeated*
3.10.1 What Is Recurrence Prevention?   59
3.10.2 Case Study: Recurrence Prevention Using
        Defect Analysis Sheets   60
3.11 Standardization   61
Formulate, observe, and utilize standards
3.11.1 What Is Standardization?   61
3.11.2 Case Study: Work Standards Specifying Key
        Points   67

**Chapter 4 The QC Seven-Step Formula—Solving Problems
the QC Way   71**

**4.1 The Significance of the QC Seven-Step
     Formula   71**
You can't get good without knowing the basics
4.2 The QC Seven-Step Formula   72
Find and address the causes
**4.3 Putting the QC Seven-Step Formula into
     Practice   75**
Move forward one step at a time
Step 1: Select Topic   75
Step 2: Understand Situation and Set
Targets   82
Step 3: Plan Activities   88
Step 4: Analyze Causes   90

xvi   CONTENTS

Step 5: Consider and Implement Counter-
measures   95
Step 6: Check Results   102
Step 7: Standardize and Establish Control   104

Chapter 5 The QC Tools   111

5.1 The Significance of the QC Tools in the QC Problem-Solving Approach   111
You can't build a house without hammer and nails

5.2 Individual QC Tools   113
The problem-solving toolbox

5.3 How to Use the QC Tools   119
A system for becoming a skillful user of the QC tools

5.4 The QC Seven-Step Formula and the QC Tools   120
Use the right tool at the right time

5.5 Using the QC Tools as Part of the QC Seven-Step Formula   123
Make good use of the seven QC tools
Step 1: Select Topic   123
Step 2: Understand Situation and Set Targets   126
Step 3: Plan Activities   127
Step 4: Analyze Causes   128
Step 5: Consider and Implement Counter-
measures   132
Step 6: Check Results   132
Step 7: Standardize and Establish Control   132

Chapter 6 Some Examples of the QC Problem-Solving Approach   137

6.1 The QC Story   137
The secret of preparing improvement activity reports

6.2 Announcing the Results of Problem-Solving Activities   139
Use presentation meetings to keep tabs on improvement and personal growth

6.3 Some Problem-Solving Case Studies   143
Learning from good examples

Case Study 1: Improving Precision of Load Capacity
Measurement for Drive Springs   145
Case Study 2: Reducing Number of Hang-Ups in
Switchboard Operation   152
Case Study 3: Ensuring Sufficient Adhesion in Direct
Application of Tiles to Concrete   160

References   165

Index   167

Figures and Tables

Figure 1.1   Role and Attitude Required of Division and Section
              Managers   4
Figure 1.2   The Meaning of TQC   10
Figure 1.3   Relationship between Problem-Solving and TQC   12
Figure 2.1   What is a Problem?   14
Figure 2.2   The Four Types of Problem   16
Figure 2.3   What is the QC Problem-Solving Approach?   18
Table 3.1   The QC Midset   21
Figure 3.1   Quality-First Activities   24
Figure 3.2   Careless Mistakes and Error-Proofing   26
Figure 3.3   Error-Proofing System for Preventing Packaging
              Errors   27
Figure 3.4   Results of Investigation of Waiting Times for Different
              Tests (Survey Period: 18–29 August 1987)   30
Figure 3.5   Analysis of Causes   31
Figure 3.6   Investigation and Implementation of Counter-
              measures   32
Figure 3.7   Confirmation of Results   33
Figure 3.8   Outline of Process   36
Table 3.2   Causes and Countermeasures   36
Figure 3.9   Pareto Chart for Errors (Survey Period: 1 month)   37
Figure 3.10 The PDCA Wheel   39
Figure 3.11 Spiraling Up   41
Figure 3.12 PDCA on the Construction Site   42
Figure 3.13 Priorities and Process of Education and Dissemination
              Activities   45
Figure 3.14 Identifying the Facts   49

xx   FIGURES AND TABLES

Figure 3.15   Cause-and-Effect Diagram for Insulation Sealing Defect
              (focusing on equipment and jigs)   50
Figure 3.16   Investigation Using Video Camera   51
Figure 3.17   The Meaning of Process Control   52
Figure 3.18   Process Management Flowsheet for Order-
              Taking   54
Figure 3.19   Control of Pile Installation Precision in Subway
              Construction   57
Figure 3.20   Recurrence-Prevention System   60
Figure 3.21   Defect Analysis Sheet   63
Figure 3.22   Example of Work Standard Showing Key Points of
              Work   68
Figure 3.23   Standardization of Flowchart Showing Key Points   69
Figure 4.1   The Problem-Solving Process   73
Figure 4.2   Problem-Solving Approaches   73
Table 4.1   The QC 7-Step Problem-Solving Formula   74
Figure 4.3   Approaches to Identifying Problems   76
Table 4.2   Problem Evaluation Chart   78
Figure 4.4   The Bathtub Manufacturing Process   81
Table 4.3   Examples of Control Characteristics   83
Figure 4.5   Understanding the Situation   87
Figure 4.6   Setting a Target   88
Table 4.4   Plan of Problem-Solving Activities   89
Table 4.5   Activity Plan   90
Figure 4.7   Analysis of Causes   93
Table 4.6   Idea-Generating Strategies   96
Table 4.7   The 4M Technique   97
Table 4.8   The 5W1H Technique   97
Table 4.9   The WUS (Waste, Unevenness, and Strain)
              Technique   98
Figure 4.8   Countermeasure Plan and Implementation   100
Figure 4.9   Check Results   103
Table 4.10   Standardize and Establish Control   108
Figure 5.1   Using Data   112
Table 5.1   An Overview of the Seven QC Tools   116
Table 5.2   QC Tools and Their Uses   117
Table 5.3   Use of the Seven QC Tools in the QC 7-Step
              Formula   121
Figure 5.2   The QC 7-Step Formula and the Seven QC
              Tools   122
Table 5.4   Basic Graphic Symbols for Process Charts   124

FIGURES AND TABLES   xxi

Table 5.5   Auxilliary Graphical Symbols for Process
             Charts   125

Figure 5.3   Description of a Process Using Process
             Symbols   125

Figure 5.4   Topic Selection Using Matrix Diagram   126

Figure 5.5   Understanding Situation Using Line Graph   127

Figure 5.6   Bar Chart Activity Plan   127

Figure 5.7   Organizing Causes on a Cause-and-Effect
             Diagram   129

Figure 5.8   Comparing Stratified Data Using Histograms   130

Figure 5.9   Investigating Time Changes Using Graphs   131

Figure 5.10 Investigation of Correlation Using Scatter
             Diagram   131

Figure 5.11 Evaluating Countermeasures Using a Systematic
             Diagram   133

Figure 5.12 Devising Countermeasures Using Idea-Generating
             Strategies   134

Figure 5.13 Checking results with Control Charts and
             Histograms   135

Figure 5.14 Establishing Control by Means of x-R_s Control
             Charts   136

Table 6.1   The QC Story and the QC 7-Step Problem Solving
             Formula   138

CHAPTER 1

The Importance of Problem Solving

Today, market needs are rapidly becoming more diversified and sophisticated, technical innovations are arriving on the scene at a bewildering pace, and competition is becoming more and more ferocious. To ride out these successive waves of change, every company now urgently requires people with a superior capacity for solving problems.

Problem-solving ability is not an inborn talent possessed by only a few special people. It is the cumulative result of individual acts and is molded and improved through repeated experience and study.

1.1 The Role of Workplace Leaders
Competent workplace leaders now required

A company is a collection of people working together to perform manufacturing, sales, or other activities, each exercising the abilities his or her role requires. For large numbers of people to be able to band together and achieve group objectives like this, some kind of management organization is needed.

Every company sets up an organization composed of structural units such as divisions, sections, and groups. Under the usual system, a leader is appointed to head up each of these organizational units. This leader is given a title such as Division Manager or Section Manager and is made responsible for directing and supervising a number of subordinates.

In this way, companies assign supervisors and managers with a variety of titles—Chief Clerk, Charge Hand, Foreman, Shift Leader, Team Leader, Work Leader, Chief Operator, Shop Manager, Office Manager, Supervisor, Group Leader, Section Manager, and so on—to oversee the places where the essential work of the organization is performed. Such managers and

1

THE QC PROBLEM-SOLVING APPROACH

supervisors are referred to throughout this book under the collective label "workplace leader." I define a workplace leader as follows:

A workplace leader is someone who has the role of managing a number of people in order to achieve certain objectives within an organization, ensuring that each individual exercises his or her full potential, and creating a workplace where everybody works together willingly to achieve results and where each person can find satisfaction in his or her work.

To achieve this, workplace leaders are given the authority they require to perform their duties and must take responsibility for fulfilling their appointed role.

In the present business climate, many companies are striving to ensure their survival by measures such as energetically promoting technical innovation, carrying out widespread organizational reforms, and shutting down unprofitable divisions. To cope with the future situation, workplace leaders must also modify their own personal abilities and working methods. It is no exaggeration to say that there has never been a time when competent, capable workplace leaders have been so urgently required.

Workplace leaders must perform a variety of tasks. Assisted by their subordinates, they must fulfill the roles described below:

(1) Unite, manage, and supervise subordinates.
   (i) Give accurate orders and instructions to subordinates.
   (ii) Assign workers to suitable tasks and share out the work appropriately according to their abilities.
   (iii) Listen carefully to subordinates' opinions and act on them.
   (iv) Pay attention to the physical and mental health of subordinates.

(2) Guide and educate subordinates.
   (i) Accurately identify subordinates' abilities and educate and train them appropriately.
   (ii) Guide subordinates in working methods and skills.
   (iii) Develop QC circle leaders.
   (iv) Evaluate the results of education programs accurately and make use of people's abilities.
   (v) Increase mutual trust in order to improve cooperation.

(3) Eliminate defects and improve quality.
   (i) Work in accordance with standards, and control processes properly.

The Importance of Problem Solving 3

   (ii) Eradicate defects, deficiencies, etc., and make excellent products without defectives.
   (iii) Improve processes to enable quality to be built in via the process.
   (iv) Plan, design, and develop new products.

(4) Reduce costs.
   (i) Produce products using specified materials, quantities, and standard times.
   (ii) Improve yields and productivity.
   (iii) Reduce number of labor-hours used through time-and-motion studies and process analysis.
   (iv) Reduce overheads by eliminating waste.
   (v) Make effective use of jigs and tools.
   (vi) Reduce stocks of materials and work-in-process.

(5) Guarantee production volumes.
   (i) Draw up daily schedules and monitor progress.
   (ii) Perform proper process allocation.
   (iii) Act to prevent stockouts or materials and parts holdups.

(6) Sell the merchandise.
   (i) Collect and analyze market information and perform new-product planning.
   (ii) Set up sales routes and agents.
   (iii) Develop strategies for securing orders and actively sell the merchandise.
   (iv) Manage the customer base.
   (v) Deal with complaints promptly and effectively.

(7) Maintain safety and create a good working environment.
   (i) Educate subordinates in safety regulations and see that they obey them.
   (ii) Ensure that periodic inspections by specialists and daily checks by workers are performed thoroughly.
   (iii) Implement and check safety measures for each process and each item of equipment.
   (iv) Institute exhaustive error-proofing measures.
   (v) If an accident does occur, take swift corrective action, compile a report, and instigate countermeasures promptly.
   (vi) Check lighting, ventilation, noise, and other working conditions.

(vii) Work hard to establish the Workplace Five "S's" (*seiri*—sorting out; *seiton*—arranging efficiently; *seiso*—checking through cleaning; *seiketsu*—personal hygiene; *shitsuke*—discipline)

(8) Create a rewarding workplace.
  (i) Develop good relations among the people in the workplace.
  (ii) Raise motivation and create a workplace with high morale.
  (iii) Master the art of leadership and become a trustworthy leader.
  (iv) Encourage people to submit plenty of suggestions.
  (v) Support subordinates' personal growth and mutual development.
  (vi) Ensure that subordinates are problem-conscious, and actively develop their problem-solving activities.

The basic roles and attitudes required of division and section managers are shown in Figure 1.1.

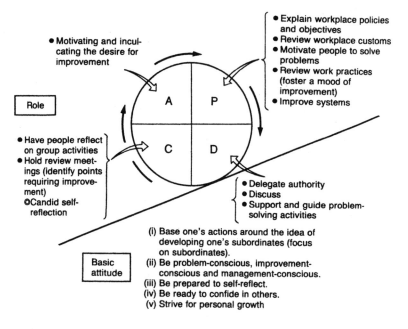

Figure 1.1 Role and Attitude Required of Division and Section Managers

The Importance of Problem Solving   5

1.2 Good Problem Solvers
Which type are you?

Life is a series of problems. Like jumping out of the frying pan into the fire, we run into one difficulty after another. Trouble is all around us. Sometimes we manage to solve a problem by exerting our utmost efforts, and this makes us happy. Sometimes we fail, and then we are depressed.

Humankind is made up of an infinite variety of people. You and I are different. No two people are alike.

When we look at attitudes toward solving problems, we find that people can be divided into the four main types described below. Into which of these categories do you fit?

Problem-Solving Types

Type 1: The self-negating, despairing type. Every time these people run across a problem, they convince themselves that they cannot possibly solve it because they lack talent and self-confidence. They tackle problems half-heartedly, constantly worry about the smallest setbacks, and blame everything on their supposed incompetence if the problem proves insoluble.

If we believe we are worthless and think, "I can't do it," or "It's impossible" whatever situation we find ourselves in, such negative thoughts are bound to turn into self-fufilling prophecies and render us useless and incapable.

The American management expert Peter Drucker says that a person who has never failed is a person who has never tried. Surely, not doing anything is the biggest failure of all?

The first step in escaping from this self-destructive, hopeless mold is to do something. Don't view things pessimistically, don't be afraid of failure; come to grips with a problem. When you confront the problem and get over the first hurdle, you will see the first rays of hope.

Type 2: The "someone else's fault" type. People of this type never reflect on their own shortcomings but always blame others. Whatever the problem, they make their minds up that some other division or person is responsible. Whenever trouble occurs, they treat it as someone else's; in solving problems, they take up the stance of an observer and never try to do anything themselves. Oblivious to their own faults, they blame their colleagues, their bosses, other divisions, or anyone else they can think of for their problems. These are the people who sit at the back heckling and loudmouthing but doing nothing constructive. Their behavior is unforgivable. Bluntly speaking, it is mean and cowardly.

6   THE QC PROBLEM-SOLVING APPROACH

A problem cannot be solved unless the people noticing it rise to the challenge of solving it themselves and take the lead in tackling it. True problem solving is impossible with the type of behavior that tries to shift the responsibility on to others.

People who are in the habit of blaming others must try grasping the nettle themselves and take the initiative in tackling problems. When they do so and manage to solve a problem that they think is somebody else's fault, they will not only surprise themselves but will also experience the wonderful feeling of having solved a problem through their own efforts.

Type 3: The "ostrich" type. This is the most common type. Like an ostrich with its head in the sand, these people think that the existing situation cannot possibly be improved. Although they obey decisions and follow the standards, they never try to break out of their present situation or to better their circumstances.

This approach works tolerably well when everything is calm and peaceful and few changes occur, but it is not very useful in times of rapid change like the present. If we merely maintain the status quo and wait passively, we will eventually fade away and disappear. This approach will neither decrease defects nor increase sales.

People of this type must realize that they are surrounded by a sea of problems, and they must cultivate a burning desire to find them and solve them. In other words, they must heighten their problem-awareness and improvement-consciousness.

Type 4: The problem-solving type. People of this type always act with a specific objective in mind, actively seek out problems to tackle, and get to grips with them positively and decisively, making light of difficulties. They are flexible in their thinking when drawing up plans for solving problems and they put all their energy into solving them.

Andrew Carnegie, once the steel king of the world, said that no matter what business you are in, it is important always to do your utmost to become the best. When, at the age of twelve, he was employed as a winder in a spinning factory, he tried to become the world's number one winder. Then, when he was delivering telegrams, he strove to become the world's best telegram delivery boy. Whatever his job, he always worked with this attitude. By continuing to do so, he reached the position he did.

Good problem solvers have their own objectives. They set these objectives slightly out of reach of their present abilities and have a burning desire to attain them. Their zeal and enthusiasm become the driving force for solv-

The Importance of Problem Solving 7

ing the problem. When we put all our efforts into solving a problem, we are bound to crack it eventually.

When people solve a problem, it gives a fillip to their confidence, and they become a little better at the art of problem solving. The next time they tackle a problem, they will choose one slightly more difficult than the previous one and will set their objectives slightly higher. As they tackle a series of problems in this way, each a bit harder than the one before, they gradually raise their problem-solving ability by increasing their experience, honing their technical skills and improving their problem-solving methods.

1.3 What Is a Strong Workplace?
Tackling more challenging problems

Our daily life and work more or less always consists of solving a continuous series of problems. Going out for a round of golf, making a product on the factory floor, or selling things in a shop could all be described as types of problem-solving behavior.

All workplaces face problems large and small. Some of the more serious ones are:

- Persistent chronic defects and intractable rework costs.
- Frequent mechanical breakdowns and failure to meet production targets.
- Failure to reduce materials losses as expected, even though action is being taken.

A strong workplace is one that recognizes problems and can take steps to solve them.

Today's workplaces are beset by numerous difficulties. Some of these are:

- People need to study fresh advances in systems and equipment, but they are too busy to do so.
- Automation is reducing the number of people in the workplace, leaving too few to form QC circles.
- Each person has his or her own particular responsibilities, and there are no common topics to tackle as a team.
- People's jobs have become more complex and they cannot solve problems without outside help.

In spite of these difficulties, we must continue to think of ways to solve

8   THE QC PROBLEM-SOLVING APPROACH

problems rather than reasons why they can't be solved, and of how to make things possible rather than what can go wrong. Saying "It's no good" or "It can't be done" will get us nowhere. We have to turn ourselves into the problem-solving type of person who is always thinking of how to improve the situation.

Nobuo Ishibashi, chairman of Daiwa House Industry, the company that developed the steel-framed house and opened the way to the manufacture of prefabricated housing in Japan, says that we must break free of existing concepts and think up original ways of tackling problems[8]. After World War II, Japan's housing shortage amounted to approximately 4,200,000 homes. By 1955, this figure had risen to around 18,200,000. And even though builders wanted to construct houses, the all-important lumber was missing. During the war, Japan had failed to carry out a proper tree-planting program and had cut down trees in great numbers without thought of replacing them. As a result, Japan's forests had been ravaged. Nobuo Ishibashi questioned whether houses had to be built of wood. It occurred to him that, since no wood was available, he should look for some material to replace it.

As he was thinking along these lines, the image of a steel pipe came into his mind. Steel was readily obtainable. He thought that if steel pipes were used instead of timber, they would absorb stresses smoothly because of their cylindrical shape, and could be used to build even stronger houses. He decided to go ahead and give it a try. This led to the birth of the steel-pipe-framed house and revolutionized Japan's housing construction.

If Mr. Ishibashi had been hung up on the belief that houses had to be made of wood (a notion that had held sway in Japan for over 2,000 years), the idea of building a house using steel pipes would probably never have occurred to him. If he had not built such a house, it would have been impossible for Japan to break free of the housing shortage. "What's wrong with a car without wheels?" "There's nothing odd about a house with wheels" —Such is Mr. Ishibashi's philosophy.

To survive in the coming times, we must not merely accumulate fragmentary knowledge but must constantly develop our own personal abilities and confront new and ever more difficult problems without being hidebound by traditional concepts.

1.4 Problem Solving and TQC
Promoting firmly grounded TQC activities

Although TQC (Total Quality Control) developed mainly in the manufacturing industry, it is now gaining ground in all types of trade, including

The Importance of Problem Solving 9

the construction industry, electrical power, and retailing. It is gradually becoming established throughout the service sector. Japanese Industrial Standard JIS Z 8101 (Quality Control Terminology) defines quality control as follows:

Quality Control

A system of means for economically producing products or services possessing the qualities that meet the purchaser's requirements.

"Quality Control" is sometimes abbreviated to "QC." In addition, since modern quality control makes use of statistical techniques, it is sometimes expressly termed "Statistical Quality Control," abbreviated to "SQC."

To perform quality control effectively, the entire staff of an enterprise from top executives down through managers and supervisors to ordinary workers must participate and collaborate in it at every stage of the enterprise's activities, including market surveys, research and development, product planning, design, preparation for production, procurement, subcontracting, manufacturing, inspection, sales, and after-sales service as well as finance, personnel affairs, and education. Quality control conducted in this way is called "Companywide Quality Control" ("CWQC" for short) or "Total Quality Control" ("TQC" for short).

[**Translator's Note:** The above definition is an unofficial translation of JIS Z 8101. For the official English translation, see "JIS Handbook 1989—Quality Control," published by the Japanese Standards Association. Readers should also note that the Japanese terms CWQC and TQC refer to what is generally called TQM (Total Quality Management) in the West.]

The Four Aspects of TQC

As can be seen from its JIS definition, TQC has the following four characteristics:

1. It is performed by all personnel. When a company practices TQC, everyone from the CEO, directors, division and section managers, chief clerks, staff, and supervisors right down to shop-floor workers must participate, and every individual must practice QC. Good products cannot be made if anybody in any division or department tries to escape his or her responsibility by saying, "QC is nothing to do with me."

2. It is performed in every division. It is vital for every division within the company organization to practice QC in order to fulfill that division's particular function. This applies to every division without exception, including general affairs, accounting, product planning, design, engineering, production, sales, and service.

3. It is performed at every stage. In providing customers with merchandise or services that they will be delighted to purchase, various steps must be taken to create such products or services. Markets must be surveyed, products must be planned, designed, manufactured, and sold, and after-sales service must be provided. Methods of practicing QC must be established and developed at each of these steps.

4. It is performed comprehensively. While TQC naturally centers on the management of quality, we must also perform cost control, production management, schedule control, safety management and personnel development simultaneously. This is how we raise our level of management and produce the goods and services that consumers want and that will keep them happy. This philosophy is illustrated in Figure 1.2.

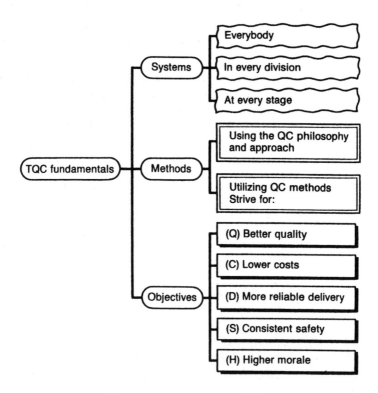

Figure 1.2 The Meaning of TQC

The Seven Features of TQC

TQC is an activity which—

1. Every employee gets involved in, from the CEO down to the lowest worker.
2. Is performed in every division within the organization, including general affairs, accounting, engineering, production, and so on.
3. Is performed at every stage of the process of providing goods and services to customers, including market surveys, product planning, design, production, sales, and after-sales service.
4. Enhances management mechanisms such as quality assurance, new-product development, cost control, production management, sales management, safety management, and personnel development, and rotates the PDCA (Plan, Do, Check, Act) Wheel.
5. Controls and improves Q (Quality), C (Cost), D (Delivery), S (Safety), and M (Morale).
6. Places great importance on the QC approach and way of looking at things.
7. Makes the use of QC methods absolutely necessary.

Of the above features, numbers 1 to 3 relate to systems, numbers 4 and 5 to objectives, and numbers 6 and 7 to methodology.

The essence of TQC is solving problems connected with quality, cost, delivery, safety, and morale. In TQC, the various management mechanisms of a company are built up around its quality assurance by the QC approach. This in turn allows the various management functions to be exercised and management objectives to be achieved. Since these management mechanisms are enhanced by standardizing the results of improvements achieved through problem-solving activities, this means that TQC and problem-solving activities are inextricably linked (see Figure 1.3).

Recently, TQC in Japan is said to have lost some of its impetus, but what this really means is that its problem-solving activities have grown weak.

THE QC PROBLEM-SOLVING APPROACH

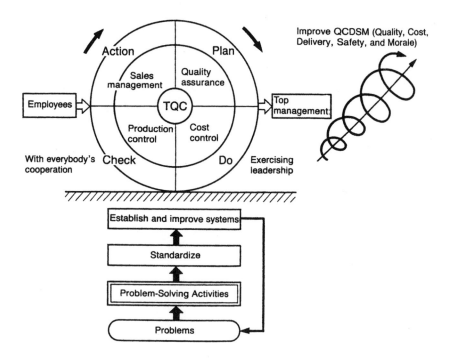

Figure 1.3 Relationship between Problem-Solving and TQC

CHAPTER 2

What Is the QC Problem-Solving Approach?

In solving problems, it is important for us to find them by ourselves and act on our own initiative. We should bear in mind the "3 Cs" (Chance, Challenge, Change), and devote all our energies to solving problems in the workplace.

The secret of skillful problem solving is to use the QC problem-solving approach. This is a formalization of the established tactics for solving problems. Its three keys are the QC viewpoint, the QC Seven-Step Formula, and the QC tools.

2.1 What Is a Problem?
Narrowing the gap between the ideal and the real

2.1.1 The Definition of a Problem

In developing our problem-solving activities, it is a good idea to start by clarifying what we mean by a problem.

We use the word "problem" all the time without really thinking about it. If suddenly asked what it means, we may find it hard to give a quick response. A simple definition might be:

• *A problem is a matter that must be resolved.*

A rather more careful definition might be:

• *A problem is a circumstance that a person has perceived consciously or subconsciously and that the person or the organization to which he or she belongs must resolve.*

THE QC PROBLEM-SOLVING APPROACH

The QC problem-solving approach defines a problem as follows:

A "problem" is the gap between the existing situation and the ideal situation or objective (see Figure 2.1).

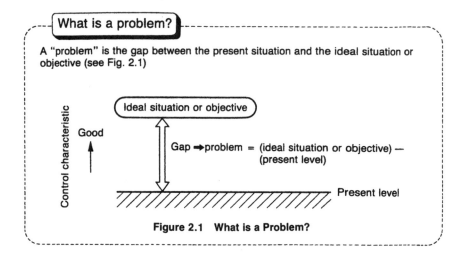

Figure 2.1 What is a Problem?

2.1.2 Classifying Problems

Problems can be classified in the following ways:

(1) According to how they come to our attention.
   (i) Everyday problems: These are the type of problems that we regularly come across while doing our jobs in the workplace. They include things such as "mechanical breakdowns" and "misassembly due to incorrect attachment of parts."
   (ii) Problems given to us to solve: This includes the type of problems that our superiors or other divisions point out to us and require us to solve. Two examples might be, "Reduce the present in-process defect rate to 1 percent" or "Cut the number of labor-hours used for assembling this part by 20 percent."
   (iii) Problems we have sought out or thought up: This is the type of problem that we actively look for and that comes to light when people begin to question the status quo and wonder whether or not it ought to be improved to even higher levels, even though things appear to be going smoothly at present. Examples might include, "Halve the time customers spend wait-

ing at the cash register," "Strengthen our system for building in quality via the process and produce fault-free products," and "Halve costs by reducing the number of parts used or replacing them with alternatives."

(2) According to the degree of obviousness of the cause and the countermeasures needed. A rather different way to classify problems is according to the obviousness of their causes and the difficulty of their solution (see Figure 2.2).

   (i) Simple problems (type C): Type C problems have simple causes, and the action needed to solve them is obvious. We can solve this type of problem by using our intelligence based on our existing knowledge, experience, and skills. Such problems include, for example, "Reduce the large numbers of wiring errors by building a wiring error detection apparatus and using it to check the wiring," or "Since the liquid temperature is not controlled at present, install thermometers and adjust the temperature based on their readings."

   (ii) Problems requiring a high level of technology (type B): A problem falls into this category if we have identified its causes from the existing conditions in the workplace but do not know how to solve it. Examples might include "Sales have dropped because a competitor has opened a new store nearby," or "The LSI yield is low because the clean room is not clean enough." Problems of this type generally require a high level of technology or equipment investment and often cannot be solved without the help of superiors or management staff.

   The thing to remember with problems of types B and C is that what we think is the cause often turns out not to be the true one. It is therefore important to collect data in order to check this.

   (iii) Problems where the necessary action is known but where care is required (type D): With problems of this type, we know what action to take but do not understand the causes. Such problems require great care. Acting in ignorance of the causes of a problem often means that we are acting against the presenting phenomenon but not eliminating the root causes. For example, a company faced with large numbers of defective electronic parts may add an aging process to its production line in order to bring defectives to light before they can cause further trouble. In this case, the true cause of the defectives has not been

THE QC PROBLEM-SOLVING APPROACH

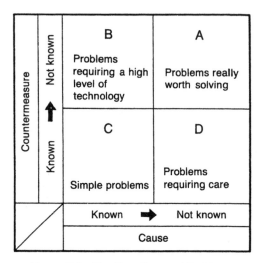

Figure 2.2 The Four Types of Problem

identified and radical recurrence-prevention measures have not been taken.

(iv) Problems really worth solving (type A): Problems of this type are extremely difficult, since neither their causes nor their countermeasures are known. This is the very type of problem that I should like workplace leaders to take up the challenge of tackling. Examples might include "Reduce the time taken to locate and extract files," "Reduce the number of assembly errors in high-speed copiers," "Reduce the time required to cook and serve a meal," or "Improve yields by eliminating waste, unevenness, and strain."

Problems of this type cannot be solved without using QC tools and pooling the talents and abilities of the group to follow the accepted QC problem-solving procedure. The benefits that accrue from solving such problems are proportional to their difficulty, and they are the best type for improving people's problem-solving skills.

What Is the QC Problem-Solving Approach? 17

2.2 A Definition of the QC Problem-Solving Approach
Use the QC approach to crack your problems

2.2.1 Problem-Solving Methods

How a problem is approached and what methods are used to solve it are immaterial as long as, in the end, it is effectively solved. However, the nature of the problem and the situation in which it arises naturally determine the best methods of addressing its solution.

As explained in the previous section using Figure 2.2, we cannot solve type A problems, where neither cause nor countermeasure is known, simply by exercising our intuitive judgment. These problems require an analytical approach. In short, the only way we can solve them is by finding their causes and devising means of eliminating these by QC techniques.

There are two main approaches to solving problems:

1. The theoretical approach. This approach, also known as the deductive method, is employed to solve problems by using relevant physical, chemical, economic, or other scientific theories, or by analogy with similar past occurrences. One example is the development of the infrared camera in order to solve the problem of how to take pictures in the dark. The infrared camera was invented by utilizing the property of infrared light, that its long wavelength makes it relatively free from dispersion by mist or water droplets in the air and that it does not easily deviate from straight paths.

2. The QC problem-solving approach. While the first approach is deductive, the QC approach could be described as inductive. In this approach, we trace the causes of the phenomenon by repeatedly asking "Why?," and identify the root causes of the problem from the facts. To solve fairly serious problems in the workplace, such as "Many defects are occurring" or "Sales are not increasing," we must apply this approach meticulously.

2.2.2 The QC Problem-Solving Approach and Its Benefits

Of the two problem-solving approaches described above, the theoretical approach is more effective when conducting basic laboratory research but the only way of effectively solving workplace problems concerning quality, cost, delivery, safety and morale (see Figure 1.2) is the QC approach. The QC problem-solving approach is undoubtedly the most effective method of solving problems in our workplaces.

So, what exactly is the QC problem-solving approach? I would like to define it here as illustrated in Figure 2.3.

THE QC PROBLEM-SOLVING APPROACH

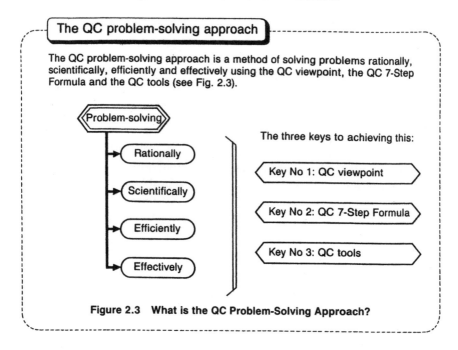

Figure 2.3 What is the QC Problem-Solving Approach?

The QC problem-solving approach is being used if the following conditions are met:

1. The reasons for selecting the topic are known and the control characteristics and objectives are clear.
2. Exhaustive analysis is being performed using QC tools.
3. Analysis has revealed a convincing relationship between the causes and the effects of the problem.
4. Ingenuity and originality are being fully exercised in devising countermeasures.
5. The QC viewpoint is being used in solving the problem.

The QC problem-solving approach makes the following ten benefits possible:

1. It enables problems to be solved more rationally, scientifically, efficiently, and effectively than any other method.
2. It heightens every person's problem-formulating and problem-solving abilities and enables everybody to fulfill an important role in the workplace.

3. It enables people to acquire the QC viewpoint through solving problems.
4. It enables people to become competent in applying the QC tools and allows them to master the scientific approach.
5. It gives tangible benefits, mainly in terms of quality, but also in terms of cost, delivery, safety, morale, sales, and so on.
6. It improves work practices and raises management standards.
7. It boosts the leadership and management abilities of workplace leaders.
8. It promotes the personal growth of individual workplace members.
9. It improves workplace communication and morale and creates cheerful, effective workplaces.
10. It stimulates QC circle and QC term activities.

2.3 The Ten Commandments for Becoming a Competent Problem Solver
Some tips for becoming good problem-solving leaders

When people form a group in order to achieve an objective, it is important for the group to work as a team and for its leader to behave like a leader, that is, to exercise leadership.

We sometimes hear of a mountain climbing expedition that meets disaster because of an error of judgment on the part of their leader or, conversely, that escapes danger thanks to their leader's good judgment. The same thing applies to solving problems: the leader's position is vital when a difficulty is faced and progress is halted.

The desire for improvement is a universal human trait, and we all have within ourselves the drive to improve our circumstances. A group leader must draw on this quality to get the group working together and lead them in the right direction. If the leader does not meet the group members' expectations in this regard, they will lose their confidence in him or her, and the group's team spirit will break down. Leaders must be responsible and courageous; they must motivate the members of their group by taking the initiative and showing their team the way.

The vital points a workplace leader must bear in mind in order to exercise leadership and dynamically promote the QC problem-solving approach can be summarized in the form of "Ten Commandments for Workplace Leaders." The QC approach will fail if any of these elements are missing. It does not matter if you cannot satisfy all of the requirements at the moment. The important thing is to advance one step at a time, little by lit-

20 THE QC PROBLEM-SOLVING APPROACH

tle, day after day, making steady progress toward new heights of achievement.

First Commandment: It is a lie to say, "We have no problems." Problems are everywhere. Actively search them out.

Second Commandment: Use accurate data, not guesswork. Observe the workplace carefully and grasp the facts accurately using data.

Third Commandment: You cannot win empty-handed. Study the QC tools well and apply them thoroughly and effectively.

Fourth Commandment: Skill is important. Improve your technical ability by studying specialist skills, techniques, and tricks.

Fifth Commandment: It is no good trying to do everything at once. Advance steadily by faithfully following the QC Seven-Step Formula.

Sixth Commandment: Do not be beguiled by apparently attractive solutions. Analyze the possible causes rigorously and only act after identifying the true ones.

Seventh Commandment: Computers are useful but not creative. Exercise your ingenuity and originality.

Eighth Commandment: Without a rational approach, things will come to a dead end. Move ahead using the QC viewpoint.

Ninth Commandment: It is no good standing back and telling your subordinates to get on with it. Tackle difficulties yourself.

Tenth Commandment: Never give up. Be determined and fight to the last.

CHAPTER 3

The QC Viewpoint—Vital for QC-Type Problem Solving

The first of the three keys to solving problems the QC way is the QC viewpoint; in other words, being QC-minded. If the QC viewpoint is lacking when formulating and solving problems, the activities will not go well.

3.1 The QC Mindset
The QC viewpoint is vital

One key to the QC problem-solving approach is to adopt the QC viewpoint. Problem-solving activities conducted without it cannot be described as QC activities. TQC has achieved such outstanding results in so many fields—not just in quality assurance and production management but also in cost control, sales management, and the workplace—because it is based on QC's uniquely rational approach.

Table 3.1   The QC Mindset

Category		The QC Mindset	Meaning
T	Total	Strengthening the company constitution	Use TQC to create a company constitution capable of achieving lasting prosperity
		Total participative management	Unite employees' talents companywide and exercise them to the full
		Education and dissemination	Boost human resource development by strengthening education and training
		QC audits	Top management itself must check the state of progress of TQC and champion TQC activities

22 THE QC PROBLEM-SOLVING APPROACH

Table 3.1—*Continued*

Category		The QC Mindset	Meaning
T		Respect for humanity	Respect people's dignity and have them do their best
S	Statistical	Use of QC tools	It's no good trying to do things by one's own devices
		Dispersion control	Pay attention to dispersion and identify its causes
Q	Quality	Quality first	Aim to secure profits by giving top priority to quality
		Consumer orientation	Make the goods and services that customers really want
		The next process is your customer	Never send defectives or mistakes on to the next process
C	Control	The PDCA Wheel	Conscientiously follow the Deming Cycle
		Management by fact	Base decisions and actions on facts
		Process control	Control the process of work rather than its results
		Standardization	Formulate, observe and utilize standards
		Source control	Control systems at their source, not downstream
		Policy management	Use policy management to evolve consistent company activities
		Cross-functional management	Create horizontal links throughout the organization and improve systems for managing quality, cost, delivery, safety and morale
I	Improvement	Priority consciousness	Pounce on priority problems and attack them mercilessly
		The QC 7-Step Formula	Effect improvements by faithfully following the QC 7-Step Formula
		Recurrence prevention, prior prevention	Never repeat the same mistake! Do not neglect recurrence prevention and prior prevention of trouble

I consider the QC viewpoint extremely important, and I have summarized it in the form of the twenty items shown in Table 3.1[2]. As mentioned above, it is vital for problem-solving activities. I have selected ten items from the table that are important for problem-solving and these are discussed in detail below.

The QC Viewpoint—Vital for QC-Type Problem Solving   23

3.2 "Quality First"
Above all, produce good quality

3.2.1 What Is "Quality First"?

Quality management is an activity designed to develop, improve, and sustain goods and services that will satisfy the customer. In the past, "cheap and nasty" was a byword for Japanese goods. It is certainly true that, in the years immediately after World War II, watches that gained or lost as much as five minutes a day, shoes that wore out after being worn a few times, radios that were hard to listen to because of their constant hissing and crackling, and other such shoddy merchandise could be seen all around.

Now, however, the picture has changed, and "Made in Japan" means "reasonably priced and of good quality." This is because Japanese manufacturers made "quality first" their company policy, introduced and promoted TQC, and worked hard to achieve their goals of producing and passing on no defectives.

So, what exactly does "quality first" mean?

"Quality first" means putting quality above everything else in order to create highly satisfactory goods and services of guaranteed quality that customers will be attracted to buy and delighted to use.

In other words, "quality first" is the philosophy of giving priority to improving quality and giving it pride of place before sales, costs, or productivity. It is based on the understanding that an uncompromising commitment to the quality-first philosophy naturally results in lower costs and higher productivity. Securing profits is of course a necessary condition for a company's development, but profits must be pursued through the quality-first approach. President Hirotaro Higuchi of Asahi Breweries, a company that shook up the Kirin-dominated Japanese beer market in 1988 and leapt from the number three position to number two after the launch of its new "dry beer," says this about the success of his company's product:

> Asahi's "dry beer" succeeded because we believed that taste is something our customers should determine, and we gave priority to using the best ingredients and choosing the right time to launch the product. Cost calculations were a secondary consideration.

Nissan Motor has succeeded in shrinking the market share of Japan's automobile market leader, Toyota. President Yutaka Kume claims that the key to his company's success lay not in trying to please its dealers, but in creating a relaxed atmosphere in which everyone strives to produce top-quality products.

THE QC PROBLEM-SOLVING APPROACH

The following points are important in turning the quality-first philosophy into reality:

"Quality-first" strategies
1. Develop complex, highly original, new technology.
2. Unearth the latent wants and needs of the marketplace and develop new types of products that will stimulate fresh demand and create new markets.
3. Improve and control processes to eliminate defects, and produce products that will function as nearly perfectly as possible.

In putting quality first, the various actions depicted in Figure 3.1 must be carried out.

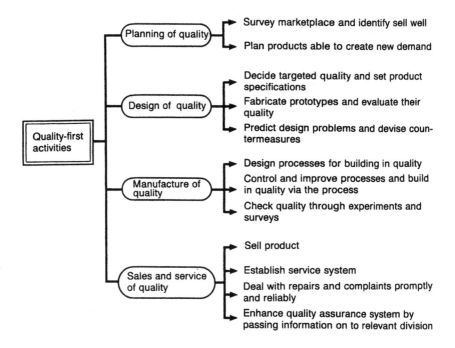

Figure 3.1 Quality-First Activities

3.2.2 Case Study: Preventing Careless Mistakes by Error-Proofing

Every Japanese workplace carries out daily improvement activities aimed at eliminating defects and deficiencies. Even so, minor slips still occasionally lead to major disasters. There is no end to the number of problems that can be caused by careless mistakes such as the following:

- Explosion caused by liquid leaking from a reactor vessel as a result of making repairs with the wrong length of bolts.
- Death by asphyxiation because of a failure to notice a gas leak on a construction site.
- Breakage of a syringe at a hospital.
- Giving the wrong change at a supermarket checkout.
- Incorrect delivery of goods by a department store.

The elimination of careless errors is an important topic in every field—not only in the manufacturing industry but also in offices, sales divisions, and service organizations.

Mechanisms designed to prevent careless errors were originally called "foolproofing devices," but this spurred complaints from workers, who resent being regarded as fools. "Error-proofing" is the preferred term nowadays. The two basic methods of error-proofing are described below.

Basic error-proofing methods

1. Create methods of working that cannot be mistaken no matter who follows them.
2. Arrange things so that, if an error occurs, either it is immediately noticed or its effect is nullified.

Figure 3.2 shows the points we should bear in mind regarding error-proofing. Figure 3.3 illustrates an example of an error-proofing system devised by the workers in the steel-cabinet workshop of the No.2 Operating Division of Itoki Crebio Corporation. "Packing the wrong number of plates" was a chronic error in the packing process for steel backplates. This error was completely eliminated by installing a weight sensor that immediately alerted the workers when the weight of a package was wrong.

THE QC PROBLEM-SOLVING APPROACH

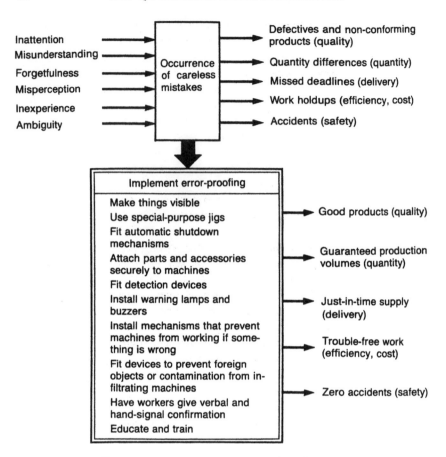

Figure 3.2 Careless Mistakes and Error-Proofing

3.3 Consumer Orientation
Make the products the customer really wants

3.3.1 What Is Consumer Orientation?
The fundamental aim of quality management is to develop, manufacture, and sell goods and services that satisfy customers and are acceptable to society. The "market-in" philosophy is essential for this.

The "market-in" philosophy means placing oneself in the users' shoes and manufacturing goods and services that meet market needs. This contrasts with the "product-out" philosophy, a manufacturer-centered approach

The QC Viewpoint—Vital for QC-Type Problem Solving 27

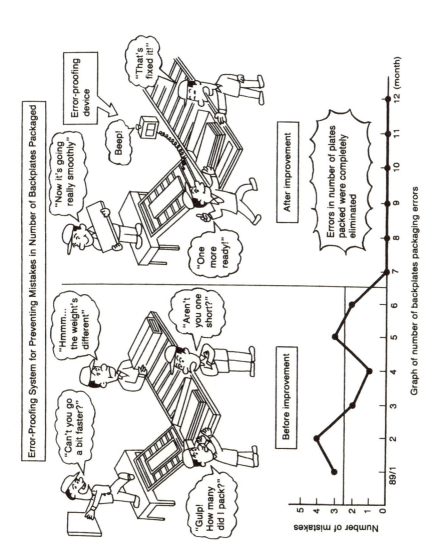

Figure 3.3 Error-Proofing System for Preventing Packaging Errors

28 THE QC PROBLEM-SOLVING APPROACH

that consists of forcing onto the market goods and services produced for the manufacturer's benefit.

To stimulate demand, promote sales, and improve services, it is essential to adopt an uncompromisingly customer-oriented approach based on the market-in concept.

Consumer orientation is the desire to produce goods and services that customers want and that they will be happy to buy.

To achieve this aim, we must take the following actions:

The three keys to consumer orientation
1. Identify market wants and needs, and plan and develop goods and services that meet them.
2. Strengthen and enhance the quality assurance system, design and manufacture products from the user's standpoint, and produce defect-free products.
3. Provide an effective after-sales service, deal with complaints promptly, and use the information obtained to prevent any recurrence.

3.3.2 Case Study: Consumer Orientation in Hospital Reception Work

The Matchbox Circle, led by Masato Matsushita in the Administration Section of Osaka's Sumiyoshi Morimoto Hospital, is in charge of outpatient and visitor reception. Every day, Mr. Matsushita and the members of his quality circle put themselves mentally in the outpatients' and visitors' shoes and think about how to interact with them in a more caring way. Let us look at this example to see how the circle interprets and puts into practice the concepts of consumer orientation and the market-in approach[10a].

Topic: Immediately take up as an improvement topic any deficiencies that have been noticed
1. My "consumer orientation"

My job is to receive visitors to the hospital, and my consumers, that is, my customers, consist of the outpatients and visitors who come to the hospital every day, as well staff from other departments in the hospital. Each of these different types of customer must be handled differently, but I always try to deal with them pleasantly, in a way that makes them feel good.

Patients are special, since coming to hospital is usually a very stressful event for them. If we reception staff treated them coldly or indifferently or told them things in an unacceptable way, what would happen?

The QC Viewpoint—Vital for QC-Type Problem Solving 29

They would simply become more and more worried. We don't have to go overboard in serving them, but we must constantly bear in mind that caring treatment is important for each individual.

2. The "consumer-oriented" mental attitude

Most people in service industries greet their customers with a polite, "Good morning. What can I do for you?" and say, "Thank you very much" when they leave. Hospital staff can also use thoughtful and considerate salutations in no way inferior to those used in other service industries. Suitable expressions might include "Good morning. What seems to be the matter?," "I hope you feel better soon," and so on. Every morning, we reception staff all gather in the reception area and chorus these greetings together to get ourselves in the right frame of mind for the day.

We also have another important role to play. This is to listen carefully to what our patients are saying. If there is anything they are unhappy about in the hospital, we must get in touch with the relevant department and remove the cause of the grievance. To succeed in this, we reception staff have to get to know our patients. Some patients may resist the idea of becoming friends with a hospital, but this is an important part of our job, since it helps to put patients' minds at rest.

3. Activities carried out and results achieved

At our hospital, we have a system where, after medical tests have been completed, the patient's medical charts return to reception, where we input the details into our computer and work out the bill.

One day, a patient criticized us severely, saying, "My tests were finished ages ago. I was told not to have anything to eat before them, and I'm still waiting for the bill. Can't you speed things up a bit?" I had also been thinking for some while that patients' waiting times might be rather long, so I mentioned this to the QC circle members and we took up the problem as an improvement topic. I would like to describe this example here.

1. Identify the topic: reducing patients' waiting times after completion of ultrasonic scanning.
2. Identify status quo (see Figure 3.4).
3. Analyze possible causes (see Figure 3.5).
4. Discuss and implement countermeasures (see Figure 3.6).
5. Check results (see Figure 3.7).
6. Standardize and establish control. Once every two weeks, the circle leader checks the waiting times and displays them on a graph.

30 THE QC PROBLEM-SOLVING APPROACH

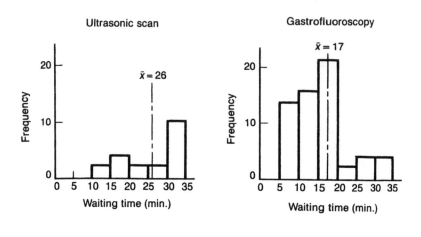

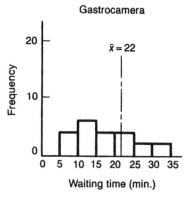

Figure 3.4 Results of Investigation of Waiting Times for Different Tests (Survey Period: 18–29 August 1987)

The QC Viewpoint—Vital for QC-Type Problem Solving

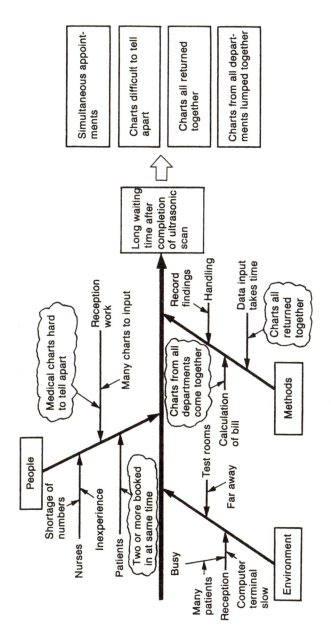

Figure 3.5 Analysis of Causes

32 THE QC PROBLEM-SOLVING APPROACH

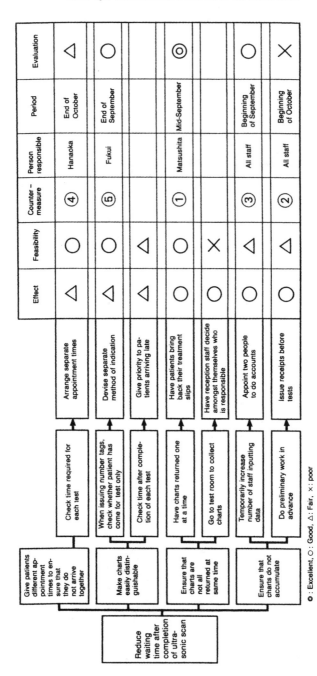

Figure 3.6 Investigation and Implementation of Countermeasures

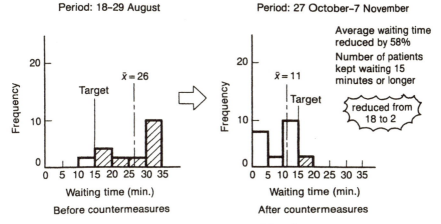

Figure 3.7 Confirmation of Results

4. Summary

We intend to go on putting ourselves in the patient's shoes in order to find improvement topics to tackle, and we will continue actively trying to improve our service.

3.4 The Next Process Is Your Customer
Never send defectives or mistakes on to the next process

3.4.1 What Does "The Next Process Is Your Customer" Mean?

Companies operate by parceling out their work among large numbers of people. This is because they adhere to the basic principle that specialization—that is, putting people in charge of particular jobs or work areas—leads to fewer errors and enables job-related techniques and skills to be accumulated.

Since our own process's output is the next process's input, the work we do must keep the people in all the processes downstream of ours, not just the next one, happy and satisfied. In other words, the idea that the next process is our customer is important.

Let us discuss what "The next process is your customer" actually means. Processes before our own are called "previous processes," while those after our own are called "next processes."

- *Previous process:* any process that affects our own work. Usually refers to processes upstream of our own.

34   THE QC PROBLEM-SOLVING APPROACH

- *Own process:* the process for which we ourselves are in charge.
- *Next process:* any process affected by our own work. Usually refers to processes downstream of ours.

Whatever work we do, there are always several "next processes." As mentioned above, "next process" means any process affected by our own work. We can rephrase the admonition, "The next process is your customer" to "Complete your work in such a way that subsequent processes will be happy to receive it."

If there is something slightly wrong with the finish of a job, or if a batch of products contains some defectives, the person who did the job or made the products is the one most likely to know about it. It is important for us to take full responsibility for our own work and to fulfill our role properly, making sure that we do not pass along such defects to the next process and satisfying ourselves that any work leaving our hands is defect-free.

"The next process is your customer" means thinking of the recipient (the next process) of the goods or services produced in one's own process as a customer and passing on to them only defect-free products or services. To achieve this, each person must perform his or her assigned duties properly before handing over to the person in charge of the next process.

The seven key points of the "next process is your customer" concept
1. Always think and act from the standpoint of the next process.
2. Understand the role of your own process well.
3. Establish good communications with previous and subsequent processes.
4. Understand the next process well.
5. Exchange accurate information through feedback and feedforward.
6. Set clear acceptance and rejection standards.
7. Perform rigorous autonomous inspection.

3.4.2 Case Study: Providing Tools that Satisfy the Next Process
The next case study is based on a presentation by Masanori Takeshita, leader of the "Rainbow Circle" in the Tool Production Section of the No.1 Production Department in Nitto Seiko's Fastener Division[10b]. It is an excellent concrete example of putting the "next process is your customer" philosophy into practice.

1. Our "next process"
We are responsible for stocking and issuing tools used for cold roll-

The QC Viewpoint—Vital for QC-Type Problem Solving   35

ing and pressing. Our customers are the people in the production section who use these tools to make screws and other rolled parts.

The most important thing in our job is to supply the tools to the next processes "just-in-time." If we fail to meet the demands of our "customers," the production plans will be disrupted and the end users will be seriously inconvenienced.

2. The mental attitude needed for the "next process is your customer" approach
   a. Check all the more carefully if you are short of time
      Our customers request tools on official "Tool Issue Request Forms." When in a hurry, however, they sometimes ask for tools by telephone or in person. On such occasions, we listen to their requests extra carefully and check that we have got it right by reading the details back to them.
   b. Practice "just-in-time"
      To ensure that we do not overstock or run out of tools, we visit the workplace whenever we have a little spare time to check how busy people are and hear what they have to say. When all is said and done, delivering 7,000 different types of tool, many similar in appearance, just in time and without error, is a formidable task. We must also be sure to observe the first-in, first-out order. We therefore try our hardest every day to achieve objectives such as "eradicate work errors," "improve product knowledge," "practice the workplace Seven S's," and "devise ways of reducing stocktaking discrepancies."

3. What we did and what we achieved!
   I would like to talk about one objective we achieved, that of eradicating work errors.
   a. Outline of process (see Figure 3.8)
   b. Occurrence of work errors
      • Length of survey—1 month
      • Total number of issues—3,920
      • Number of errors—112
      • Number of different types of error—see Figure 3.9 (before improvement)
   c. Causes and countermeasures (see Table 3.2)
   d. Results (surveyed under same conditions as before improvement)
      • Length of survey—1 month
      • Total number of issues—3,818

THE QC PROBLEM-SOLVING APPROACH

- Number of errors—14
- Situation before and after improvement—see Figure 3.9

Figure 3.8 Outline of Process

Table 3.2 Causes and Countermeasures

Work error	Main cause	Countermeasure
Errors in filling out tool request forms	Many incorrect computer codes and symbols • Customer does not know correct code or symbol • Number of spaces on request form does not match number of characters in code (number of characters differs depending on type of tool)	Prepare chart showing computer codes and symbols and display this at issuing desk Improve request forms (change code boxes, etc.) Request cooperation from production sections and subcontractors
Wrong tool issued	Inadvertent mistakes • Product mix has changed and old storage arrangements are no longer suitable • Many different types of tool handled • Many tools look almost the same • Some have lost their serial number label • Some very similar tools are mixed together • New workers do not know the correct storage locations	Decide new storage arrangements Change serial number labels to new type Sort through tools and arrange efficiently Prepare storage location chart Confirm serial number verbally when taking out tools
Wrong quantity issued	Mistakes occur when large numbers of small tools are issued	Count large numbers of small tools twice
Incorrectly completed delivery notes	Serial number is often written incorrectly, e.g. B is written instead of A	Confirm verbally
Despatch error	Crates mixed up Wrong address stamped on crate	Confirm verbally Store address stamps by area in order of frequency of use

The QC Viewpoint—Vital for QC-Type Problem Solving

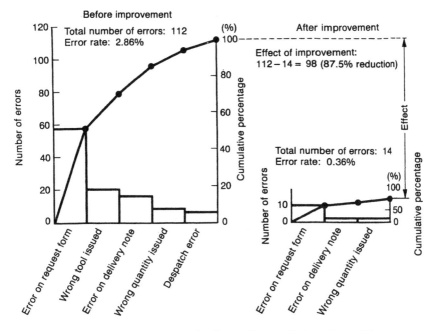

Figure 3.9 Pareto Chart for Errors (Survey Period: 1 month)

e. Summary

As a result of the great reduction in work errors, our "customers" tell us that things have got much better recently. This has made us all the more satisfied with what we are doing. We want to use this as a stepping-stone to develop our "next process is your customer" activities even further and eliminate these errors entirely.

3.5 The PDCA Wheel
Rotate the PDCA wheel diligently

3.5.1 What Is Management?

The word "management" is used in various fields: besides quality management, it is also used in cost management, personnel management, subcontractor management, and so on. In addition to the activity of managing, it also means the job or occupation of manager and is a collective term for managers themselves.

THE QC PROBLEM-SOLVING APPROACH

I would like to define "management" here as *those activities needed for continuously, rationally, and efficiently performing a job and achieving an objective.*

When managing anything, it is important to take the following four steps:

Step 1: Prepare a plan (*Plan*).
Step 2: Implement the plan (*Do*).
Step 3: Check the results (*Check*).
Step 4: Take action based on the findings of Step 3 (*Act*).

These four steps make up the PDCA (Plan–Do–Check–Act) Wheel, also known as the Deming Cycle.

What is the PDCA wheel?

When we arrive at our office or factory in the morning, we are probably thinking along the following lines:

• What job do I have to do today?
• What do I have to do in order to perform it?

We also probably make decisions like the following:

• I think I'll do this job today by such and such a procedure.
• Since we ran into these problems the other day, I'll do it by this method today and avoid causing the same trouble.

This constitutes our plan for the day's work. It is the "Plan" part of the PDCA Wheel.

Then, in accordance with our plan, we perform actions such as the following:

• Prepare documents.
• Process forms.
• Perform assembly work.

Such actions constitute the "Do" part of the PDCA Wheel.

Let us imagine that it is now noon, and we have only completed half the amount of work we planned to do. If we look back at our morning's work during the lunch break and ask ourselves why we were only able to do half of what we intended, we may come up with reasons such as the following:

- Mechanical trouble occurred and the equipment stopped working.
- We were given an unplanned rush job to do.
- We had planned more work than we could manage.

This is the "Check" phase of the PDCA Wheel. In this phase, we review the contents of our morning's plan.

In the afternoon, we may try to catch up on our schedule and complete the work we were unable to finish in the morning. We may attempt to do this by means such as the following:

- Try a different method of working.
- Make a bit more effort and increase our efficiency.
- Ask someone else to help us if it is obvious that we cannot meet today's deadline on our own.

This constitutes the "Act" phase of the PDCA Wheel.

We have all gone through this kind of process subconsciously during the course of our daily work. When we do so, we are in fact rotating the PDCA Wheel.

In our management activities, it is important to rotate the PDCA Wheel, as shown in Figure 3.10.

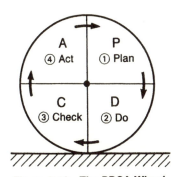

Figure 3.10 The PDCA Wheel

The PDCA Wheel is a step-by-step method of getting things done effectively and reliably. It consists of drawing up a plan, implementing the plan, checking the results, and taking any necessary corrective action.

In other words, it is important to repeat the Plan–Do–Check–Act series of steps continually in our management activities. Rotating the PDCA Wheel is the best way of managing any job.

40 THE QC PROBLEM-SOLVING APPROACH

Let us look at each of the four steps in a little more detail.

Step one: Draw up a plan (Plan)
When drawing up a plan, the following three points are important:

1. Clarify the objectives and decide on the control characteristics (control items).
2. Set measurable targets.
3. Decide on the methods to be used to achieve the targets.

Step two: Implement the plan (Do)
This step can be broken down into the following three phases:

1. Study and train in the method to be used.
2. Implement the method.
3. Collect data on the quality characteristics using the method decided.

Step three: Check the results (Check)
In this step, we check progress and evaluate the results obtained:

1. Check whether the work has been performed according to the standards.
2. Check whether the various measured values and test results meet the standards.
3. Check whether the quality characteristics match the target values.

Step four: Take corrective action (Act)
Take action based on the results of the investigation performed in step three:

1. If the work deviates from the standards, take action to correct this.
2. If an abnormal result has been obtained, investigate the reason for it and take action to prevent it recurring.
3. Improve working systems and methods.

It is important to rotate the PDCA Wheel and follow the above four steps steadily and faithfully.

Although the PDCA Wheel consists of four steps, there is a tendency to take it only as far as the "Do" step. However, we will never achieve good results if we only pay attention to what is in front of our noses. In QC, particular emphasis is placed on planning carefully, checking the results of implementing the plan, and taking any necessary corrective action.

The aim of this is to raise the standard of our work in a continuous upward spiral by faithfully rotating the PDCA Wheel, reflecting on our achievements, and taking action to improve the way we do things the next time (see Figure 3.11).

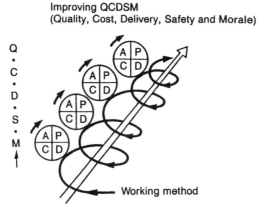

Figure 3.11 Spiraling Up

3.5.2 Case Study: PDCA on a Construction Site

Maeda Construction Co., Ltd. aims to become a major all-round construction company based on its management policy of "winning customer confidence through high-quality work." All its actions stem from its corporate motto, "Integrity, Enthusiasm and Technology." This company established the site management system shown in Figure 3.12 after realizing the enormous impact that site management methods at the construction stage have on the quality of the finished structure. This system allows the company's branch offices, site offices, and subcontractors to work in close contact with each other for sound management of the construction work and has improved the QCDSM (Quality, Cost, Delivery, Safety, and Morale) levels built into each stage of the process.

THE QC PROBLEM-SOLVING APPROACH

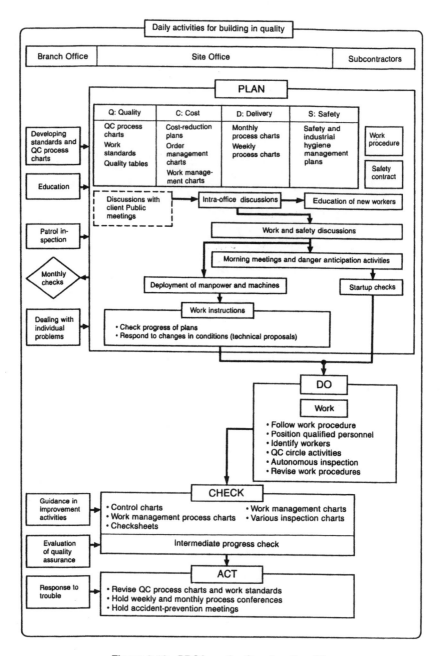

Figure 3.12 PDCA on the Construction Site

The QC Viewpoint—Vital for QC-Type Problem Solving 43

3.6 Priority Consciousness
Pounce on priority problems and attack them mercilessly

3.6.1 What Is Priority Consciousness?

Workplaces are filled with problems. There are countless potential pitfalls lying in wait to trap us and make our work turn out badly. It is vital to take action to solve these problems, but limited time and resources make it impossible for us to tackle them all. Neither would it be efficient to do so. This means that we must seek out those factors that exert a big influence on the final result and take action to deal with them. In other words, rather than working on the many trivial problems, it is important to select the vital few and eliminate these.

Being priority conscious means noticing and attacking problems whose solution will result in significant improvements.

Being priority conscious means:

1. Realizing that although various problems may exist, there are only a very few really important ones.
2. Understanding that if we address and solve the priority problems, we will obtain much better results for the same amount of effort.

The term "priority problems" refers to problems of the type described below:

1. Factors whose elimination or improvement will assist us significantly to achieve our targets.
2. Items whose improvement or elimination is thought necessary for strengthening the company's organization in the future.
3. Obstacles to the achievement of management objectives.
4. Those lower-level targets devolved from higher-level objectives that must be treated as a priority.
5. Troublesome matters whose improvement or elimination is regarded as being particularly essential if targets are to be achieved.
6. Important factors thought to have a significant influence on vital quality characteristics.

3.6.2 Case Study: Priority Consciousness in Education and Dissemination

Itoki Crebio Corporation, a general manufacturer with a product line con-

THE QC PROBLEM-SOLVING APPROACH

sisting of office furniture and equipment, industrial equipment, and household furniture, is aiming to expand its operations under the management policy, "Contributing to social progress by supplying reliable products and services that will please customers."

The company's education and training is basically planned by the management division at its head office and developed and implemented by individual operating divisions. Before the company introduced TQC, it encouraged its employees' self-development through correspondence courses, occasional courses given by specialists, and training programs for employees at different levels of the company hierarchy, but it experienced the following problems:

1. Levels of problem consciousness and improvement ability were low, and too much reliance was still placed on experience and intuition in many areas.
2. There was a noticeable lack of specialized knowledge and specific technology.
3. There was little enthusiasm for participative management and improvement activities, and self-directed activities were lackluster.

After introducing TQC, the company narrowed its education and training priorities down to the following three, based on the fundamental approach of "developing personnel able to act positively with a vigorous pioneering spirit."

1. Promote QC education with the aim of improving problem-solving abilities.
2. Enhance specialized education with the aim of improving technical abilities.
3. Promote QC circle activities and suggestion schemes with the aim of revitalizing the workplace.

Concentrating on these priorities, the company implemented QC and specialist education and training programs systematically for each hierarchical level and strove to improve its overall QC problem-solving ability.

As a result, the company secured the many tangible benefits illustrated in Figure 3.13, while people learnt to understand QC methods better and became more familiar with the QC philosophy and viewpoint. In addition, every employee became more confident and positive in tackling problems.

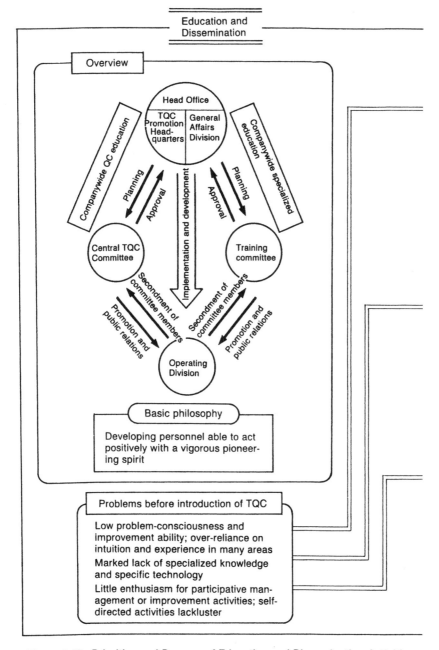

Figure 3.13 Priorities and Process of Education and Dissemination Activities

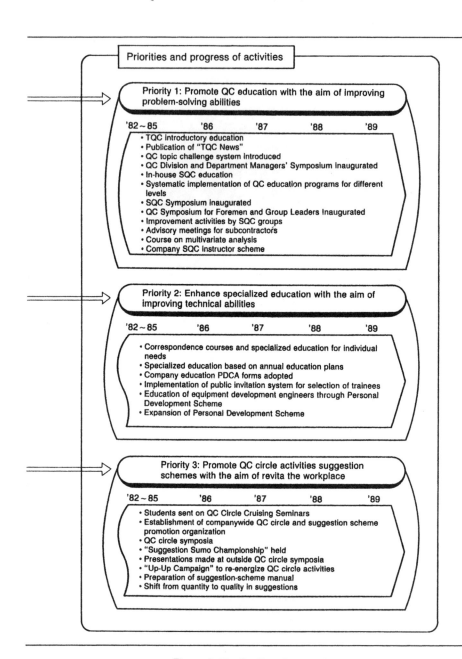

Figure 3.13—*Continued*

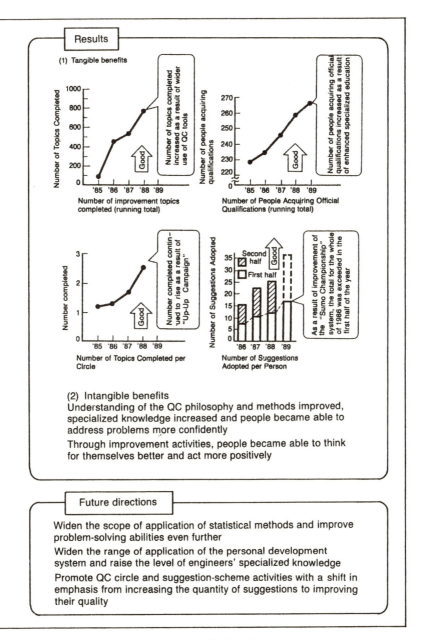

Figure 3.13—*Continued*

3.7 Management by Fact
Speak with facts and data

3.7.1 What Is "Management by Fact"?

In QC, we try as far as possible to make our various judgments based on the facts, not on guesswork. Our slogan is "Speak with Facts."

When we are born into this world, we encounter various events and meet with new experiences daily. The experience we accumulate is important; it is a valuable asset for us. However, we cannot experience everything even if we spend a lifetime trying. Even when we reach the age of forty or fifty, we are still faced with work we have never done before.

I expect most readers will have had the experience of being unable to reach a conclusion about some matter that immediately became obvious once the facts were checked. Overreliance on experience, intuition, and gut feelings is a surefire way of increasing waste.

If we are to take the correct action, it is essential to have a constant, accurate grasp of the facts. When we go out and collect data, new facts come to light, and it often becomes clear that our vague guesses based on experience were way off the mark. Checking the facts enables us to devise effective countermeasures leading to good results. It is important to be constantly in command of the facts and to accept them for what they are.

"Management by fact" means not making decisions based on experience and intuition alone but acting in accordance with the facts.

In order to base our decisions and actions on the facts, we must first quantify the situation in the form of data and convert our subjective judgments to objective ones. In identifying the facts, it is important to follow the procedure described below (see Figure 3.14).

Identifying the facts
Step 1: Closely observe the actual location and actual objects.
Step 2: Decide on the characteristics to be investigated.
Step 3: Clarify the objectives of collecting the data.
Step 4: Collect accurate data.
Step 5: Carefully analyze the data using QC tools.
Step 6: Consider the results and produce accurate information.

The QC Viewpoint—Vital for QC-Type Problem Solving

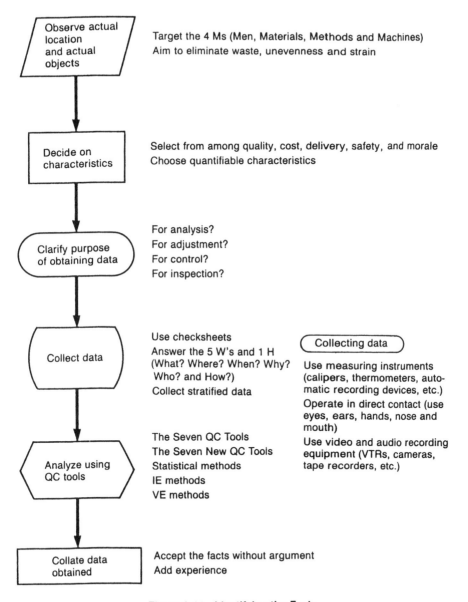

Figure 3.14 Identifying the Facts

3.7.2 Case Study: Reconstructing Defect Generation Mechanism by VTR[10d]

In an automatic assembly process for the brush holders of automobile starter motors, a defect was occurring in which the insulation was slipping out of position. The parts dimensions were all satisfactory, and it was decided, since it was an automatic process, to concentrate on finding the cause in the machinery and jigs and to review these thoroughly. A cause-and-effect diagram relating to the machinery and jigs was drawn up (Figure 3.15). The following checks were carried out:

1. Pallets were numbered and checked to see whether any were tilted.
2. The cylinder speeds of the jigs were varied and various tests were performed.

However, no definite differences were found. At this time, one of the circle members expressed the opinion that since the workstation in question was on the opposite side of the workplace, it was impossible to observe it as closely as he would like. The circle members discussed this problem and decided to investigate the defect generation mechanism using a VTR, as shown in Figure 3.16.

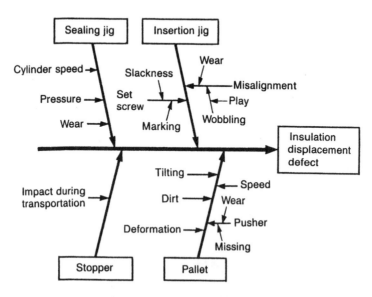

Figure 3.15 Cause-and-Effect Diagram for Insulation Sealing Defect (focusing on equipment and jigs)

The QC Viewpoint—Vital for QC-Type Problem Solving 51

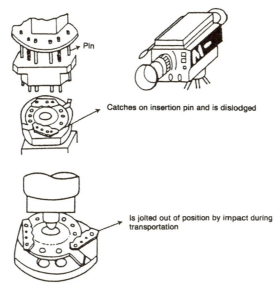

Figure 3.16 Investigation Using Video Camera

When the video was replayed in slow motion at the QC circle meeting that day, the members were able to see what the true causes of the problem were:

1. When the insulation was inserted into the plate and lifted up, it was catching on the insertion pins and being dislodged.
2. Because of its lightness, the insulation was being jolted out of position when the pallets were moved.

Improving the jigs based on the results of the above investigation enabled the problem of insulation displacement to be solved.

3.8 Process Control
Control working methods, not results

3.8.1 What Is Process Control?
When people first start to practice QC, they often think they have to obtain results quickly. Because of this, they tend to talk about the results rather than the process, making comments like the following:

- "The number of defects isn't going down. What's gone wrong?"
- "Although we've given strict orders for the objectives to be achieved, we still can't meet our sales targets."
- "I've told them time and time again to follow the safety procedures, but they still allowed an accident to happen."

In this way, people tend to concentrate exclusively on the results and forget about the process that produces them. But good results cannot be obtained until a good process has been established. The problem is not the result but the process.

The important thing in QC is to manage the processes by which we perform our various jobs and keep them in a state of control. Trying to deal with the situation after large numbers of defectives have been produced, an accident has occurred, or other trouble has arisen is like shutting the gate after the horse has bolted.

Process control means not merely chasing results but paying attention to the process (i.e., the method of working), controlling this, and improving our working systems and methods.

In other words, process control is controlling the process of the work, not running after its results (see Figure 3.17). The word "process" normally refers to the methods and actions leading up to a result. The points described below are important in process control:

Key points for process control
1. Dissect and improve present working methods.
2. Pay attention to standardization; standardize the best working methods, teach the standards, and see that these are observed.

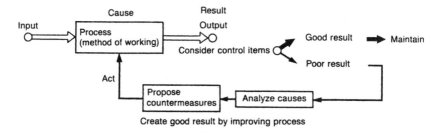

Figure 3.17 The Meaning of Process Control

The QC Viewpoint—Vital for QC-Type Problem Solving 53

3. Quality is built in via the process, not through inspection. This is what makes it so important to control processes properly.
4. Look beyond the results, reflect on the process that produced them, improve working methods, and raise the quality of work.
5. Analyze the reasons for any shortfalls between targets and results and control the cause-and-effect system.

3.8.2 Case Study: Process-Oriented Sales in Order Management

Daihen is a company that manufactures mechatronics products—mainly transformers and their associated power distribution equipment, electric welding machines, plasma cutters, and arc-welding robots. The company aims to use the introduction of TQC as an opportunity to boost its orders by accurately identifying diversifying customer needs, developing more process-oriented sales activities, and opening up new markets.

Figure 3.18 shows a flowsheet used for managing the order-taking process and increasing the number of orders obtained for product Y[5]. This sheet facilitates sales-strategy development by systematizing the entire process from obtaining information about the conditions under which a potential customer will place an order right up to actual receipt of the order. It covers every step along the route from initial approach to signing a contract, and clarifies the strategies to be taken at each step. It is used for planning follow-up action and has yielded excellent results.

The features and benefits of this "Process Management Flowsheet for Order-Taking" are as follows:

1. It systematizes the process of obtaining an order using the PDPC (Process Decision Program Chart) method (one of the Seven New QC Tools), so activities are no longer missed out.
2. It spells out the line of attack at each step and clarifies the aim of each activity.
3. It lists effective strategies for each stage of the activities, clearly specifying the action to be taken.
4. It provides space for progress to be recorded (when each step is completed, the form is marked with a different color and the completion date is noted), allowing the status of the process to be seen at a glance.
5. It sets a defined pattern for the process, eliminating the variation in activities undertaken by different sales personnel. It has also brought a greater degree of standardization to the information exchanged within the division and has made it easier to formulate strategy.

54 THE QC PROBLEM-SOLVING APPROACH

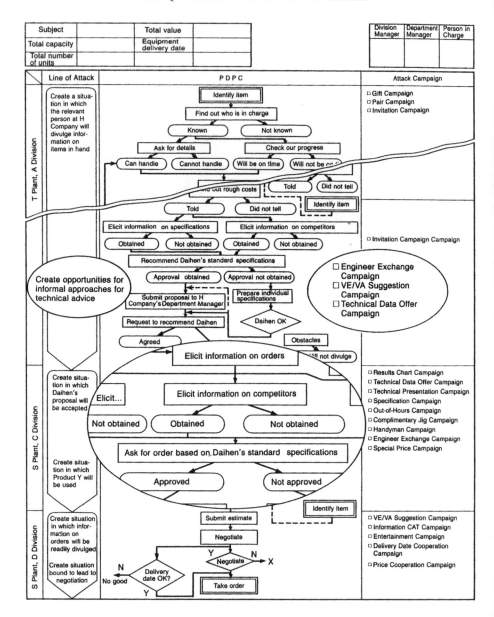

Figure 3.18 Process Management Flowsheet for Order-Taking

The QC Viewpoint—Vital for QC-Type Problem Solving 55

3.9 Dispersion Control
Pay attention to dispersion and identify its causes

3.9.1 What Is Dispersion Control?
We exert constant efforts every day to make good-quality products. However, there will always be variation in the quality of products even when the same worker makes them by the same process, according to the same work standards, using the same materials and equipment. Whatever attribute we measure—the tensile strength of steel plates, the dimensions of parts, the time taken to answer the telephone, the daily sales figures—there will always be dispersion in the data.

This is because such data are obtained from processes that we cannot perfectly control and that are affected by changes in the environment and other conditions. We are forced to accept that any data are bound to contain a certain amount of dispersion. The challenge is to keep this dispersion within acceptable limits.

Data will always be dispersed around a certain central value. We must take note of the mean and the dispersion, search out the causes of the dispersion, reduce the dispersion and keep it within acceptable limits, and maintain the process in a stable state. This is dispersion control.

There are two key points in dispersion control, as described below:

The Key Points of Dispersion Control
1. Eliminate deviation from standards.
Since data are dispersed about a certain central value, we must identify the following factors:

    i. The shape of the distribution
    ii. The central value of the distribution (the mean, $\bar{x}$).
    iii. The dispersion in the data (the standard deviation, s).

If there is any deviation from the standard, we must investigate the causes and take countermeasures. One tool we can use for comparing results with standards is the histogram.

2. Keep the process in a stable state.
Every process contains a large number of factors that create dispersion in the quality of the product. These factors or causes can be classified into the following two types:

56   THE QC PROBLEM-SOLVING APPROACH

 i. Chance causes: dispersion due to chance causes is unavoidable. It arises even when the materials, working methods, and other conditions all conform to standards.
 ii. Assignable causes: dispersion due to assignable causes must not be ignored. It arises for various reasons, such as because the work standards are not being observed or because the standards are inadequate.

To maintain a process in the stable state, we can ignore the chance causes but we must eliminate any assignable causes and take appropriate action to ensure that the same causes do not arise again in the future.

Control charts are used to analyze and control processes by classifying dispersion into the kind due to chance causes and the kind due to assignable causes.

3.9.2 Case Study: Controlling Pile Installation Precision in Subway Construction

Increasing the pile installation precision in soil–mortar walls in subway construction is extremely effective in reducing the amount of concrete used in the subsequent waling process and ensuring that the waterproof concrete is of the requisite thickness (see Figure 3.19).

In this study, groups of five piles were selected at random from each batch installed during the period September 17–October 4, and their installation precision was measured. The results are shown in Figure 1. In Figure 2, the deviations of the pile positions from the centerline of the pile row can be seen to fall more or less within the allowed tolerance. On the $\bar{x}$ control chart of Figure 1, however, subgroups 5 and 18 lie outside the control limits.

A cause-and-effect diagram was therefore prepared and the method of installation was reexamined. It was realized that, since the piles are "floating" in the soil–mortar mixture immediately after installation, they are unstable and easily disturbed by work done in the adjacent construction section. The problem was seen to lie in the method of fixing the piles in position and the order in which the work sections were tackled.

The countermeasures illustrated in Figures 3–5 were therefore applied, and a fresh $\bar{x}$–R chart (Figure 6) and histogram (Figure 7) were drawn up to check the outcome. Both the $\bar{x}$ and R charts showed a state of control, and the process capability index Cp had increased to 1.14, showing that the pile installation precision had improved.

The QC Viewpoint—Vital for QC-Type Problem Solving   57

| Identify Situation |

The results shown below were obtained on group of 5 piles picked at random from each batch installed during the period 17 September–4 October

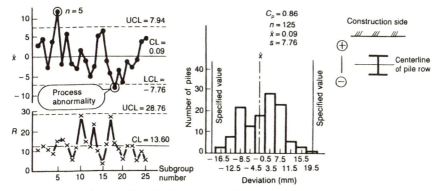

Figure 1 $\bar{x}$-R Control Chart for Pile Installation Precision

Figure 2 Histogram for Pile Installation Precision

| Consider and Implement Countermeasures |

① Improvement of method of fixing pile heads
The precision was improved by fixing the pile heads in place with an angle bar to prevent them moving out of position after installation

② Improvement of construction section sequence
The order of construction was changed to minimize disturbance by adjacent construction work

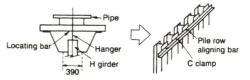

Figure 3 Method of Fixing Pile Heads

Figure 4 Change in Construction Sequence

③ Guide plate improvement
Guide plates were provided with H-shaped cutouts to ensure that the H-section girders remained in close contact with the guide plates during pile installation. This stopped the H-section girders from vibrating during installation.

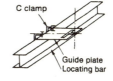

Figure 5 Guide plate

Figure 3.19 Control of Pile Installation Precision in Subway Construction

THE QC PROBLEM-SOLVING APPROACH

> Check Results

During the period 6-30 October, groups of 5 piles were selected at random from each batch as before, and control charts and a histogram were prepared.

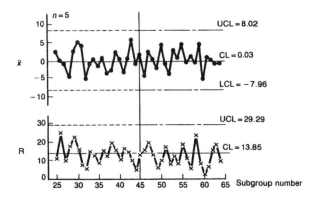

Figure 6 $\bar{x}$-R Control Chart for Pile Installation Precision (After Improvement)

The post-improvement control charts and histogram show the following benefits:
① The waterproof concrete in the subsequent process is of the required thickness
② The quantity of concrete behind the waling has been reduced
③ The appearance is satisfactory

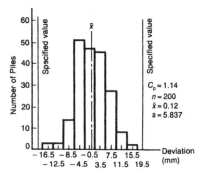

Figure 7 Histogram for Pile Installation Precision (After Improvement)

Figure 3.19—*Continued*

The QC Viewpoint—Vital for QC-Type Problem Solving   59

3.10   Recurrence Prevention

Institute radical countermeasures to ensure that the same mistake is not repeated

3.10.1   What Is Recurrence Prevention?

From any point of view, maintaining processes in a stable state is the basis of a healthy production system. However, trouble often occurs even when we do our best to maintain our processes in the stable state. This happens for reasons such as the following:

- Worker inattention.
- Equipment failure.
- Contamination of raw materials and processes by impurities, dust, and other foreign matter.
- Mistakes in following work procedures.

By "trouble" I mean anything that actually causes harm or is thought likely to cause harm in the future.

Stopgap measures alone are inadequate for dealing with trouble. A countermeasure is only really effective if it prevents the trouble from recurring.

Recurrence prevention means identifying the causes of trouble and taking countermeasures against those causes to ensure that they never recur.

Many of the workplace countermeasures adopted in areas such as design, manufacturing, sales, and service are no more than first-aid measures aimed at suppressing the symptoms. The problem is that in only a very few cases is the action carried far enough to prevent the trouble recurring. It is essential to identify the causes of problems and take action against them.

To achieve this, the following three types of countermeasure must be taken (see Figure 3.20).

Countermeasure types

Type 1: Emergency countermeasures

These are makeshift remedies designed to deal with the immediate trouble—for example, changing the method of adjustment, introducing screening inspection, changing the method of operation, and so on.

Type 2: Individual recurrence-prevention countermeasures (permanent countermeasures)

These are permanent countermeasures for dealing with trouble arising

THE QC PROBLEM-SOLVING APPROACH

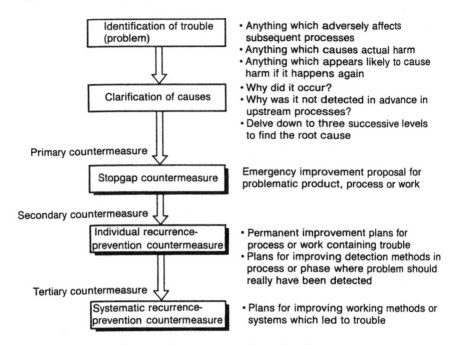

Figure 3.20 Recurrence-Prevention System

in products, processes, and work. They are aimed at either the work or process that created the problem or the method of detection that allowed the problem to go unnoticed. Examples include correcting a die, changing a thickness, or changing a material.

Type 3: Systematic recurrence-prevention countermeasures

These are countermeasures designed to improve the system aspect of working methods, mechanisms, and so on (procedures, technical standards, control standards, organizations, job sequences, and the like) in order to prevent the recurrence of trouble due to the same cause.

3.10.2 Case Study: Recurrence Prevention Using Defect Analysis Sheets

When defects occur within a process or complaints are received from the marketplace, it is vital to take appropriate steps to trace their causes and carry out systematic countermeasures. Figure 3.21 shows a "Defect Analysis Sheet" used for this purpose.

Using these sheets, the causes of the trouble are traced down to three

The QC Viewpoint—Vital for QC-Type Problem Solving　　　61

successive levels, and emergency countermeasures, individual recurrence-prevention countermeasures, and systematic recurrence-prevention countermeasures are taken against the causes. The lower part of the form lists various possible causes of trouble, facilitating their speedy and accurate identification.

3.11　Standardization
Formulate, observe, and utilize standards

3.11.1　What Is Standardization?

Quality control and standardization are extremely closely linked. Inadequate standardization leads to the following problems:

- Mistakes in assembly processes, leading to the production of useless products.
- Errors in dispatching goods to customers, leading to complaints.
- Mistakes in arranging for the repair of copying machines, greatly prolonging their downtime and inconveniencing customers.

To ensure that work proceeds smoothly in a workplace, its role in the organization and the correct methods of working must be clearly specified and put down on paper so that the job can be done properly by anyone who follows the instructions. This is the whole point of standardization.

We could probably manufacture and sell products even without standardization. Without it, however, our work would contain a high degree of dispersion, we would be unable to obtain stable quality, and the work itself would be very wasteful and trouble-prone. Businesses must unify, simplify and standardize the 4 M's (Materials, Machines, Manpower, and Methods) in such a way that the work can be performed identically whoever does it and whenever it is done, and so that waste, unevenness, and strain do not arise.

The terms "standard" and "standardization" are generally used fairly loosely, but the official English translation of Japanese Industrial Standard JIS Z 8101 defines them as follows:

Standard
An agreement established for an object, performance, capability, arrangement, state, action, sequence, method, procedure, responsibility, duty, authority, way of thinking, conception, etc., for the purpose of unification and simplification so that profit or convenience may be obtained with fairness among the people concerned.

Standardization
The systematic activities of establishing and utilizing standards.

THE QC PROBLEM-SOLVING APPROACH

Issued by (person in charge, quality control department)	Person in charge, responsible division	Received	Approved	Designated date for reply to counter-measure proposal
		Person in charge, quality control dep.	QA Manager	20 August 1989
Yamada 12, June	Matsubara 19, June	Komori 21, June	Kawamura 22, June	

	Item no.	HVM5-4AK
Defect Analysis Sheet	Details	Mis-wired control cables (mis-wiring of 2 and 3)

Nature of problem	Direct cause of problem (primary) →	Why? (cause of problem at left—secondary cause)
1 Manual switching inoperative 2 Electromagnetic switching inoperative 3 Self-opening 4 Phase disconnection 5 Short-circuit 6 Grounding	**WHY** — **Mis-wiring** → Wires not crossed before soldering	An inadvertent error was made when soldering because the wires should be crossed on one side but not on the other. Soldering of wires on crossed and uncrossed sides was done unsystematically.
7 Overheating 8 Melting 9 Defective operating characteristics	Wires crossed before soldering	As above As above
10 Defective timelimit characteristics	Holes 1 and 2 should be used when mounting insulation on jig, but holes 1 and 3 were used by mistake.	Insulation was mounted with jig not in precribed position
11 Abnormal sound 12 Defective display	**Missed when checking** — Checker display lamps are hard to see	Lamp is dim
13 Insulation defect 14 Defective pressure-resistance 15 Abnormal actuating force 16 Incorrect installation of parts	Unchecked items were mistaken for checked ones when checking after soldering.	Many cables are hanging on the trolley, and the checker is moved about to perform the checks
17 Open circuit (18 Mis-wiring)	Unchecked items were mistaken for checked ones when checking wiring.	As above
19 Deformation 20 Water penetration 21 Gas leakage 22 Defective painting (insufficient thickness, surface damage) 23 Rusting 24 Other	**Faculty checker** — Checker was inspected, but no abnormality was found (when a deliberately mis-wired product was tested, the checker display lamp did not light, so there is nothing wrong with the checker). There have been no checker breakdowns in the past	—

Figure 3.21   Defect Analysis Sheet

The QC Viewpoint—Vital for QC-Type Problem Solving

Date of reply	Complaint no.	Q-SE6101		Filing no.	KA61-139
20 August 1989	Product inspection defect no.	JS-128			
	Report no.	JP-135			

Type of trouble	○ Customer complaint (serious) ○ Customer complaint (general)	☑ Product inspection defect ○ Other	Date of occurrence: 3 August 1989 Date received: 11 August 1989 Date confirmed: 11 August 1989

→	Why? (cause of problem at left—tertiary cause)		Countermeasure Clearly answer the 5W's and 1H	Date of implemen-tation	Person responsible
	(A) Wires were soldered in red-black-white order instead of red-white-black. (B) Because of the design of the product, the white and black wires must be crossed over on the reverse side.	Emergency countermeasures	Check wiring of completed and in-process products Give thorough instructions to workers to perform wiring and checking carefully	20 Aug. 12 Aug.	Quality Control Department Murayama
	(C) The jig display is hard to see (D) The product is not put down with the crossing and non-crossing sides facing in a set direction	Individual recurrence prevention measures	1. (A), (C), (E), (G)—Display colors (red, black and white) on jig 2. (D), (H)—Specify in work standards that soldering should be performed on non-crossing side first	8 Sept. 20 Aug.	Murayama Kamida
	(E), (F) and (G) as above ((A), (B) (C))		3. (I), (J), (K)—Equip jigs with pins to fix orientation of insulation	8 Sept.	Kamida
	(H) as above (D)		4. (L)—Fit shades to lamps and change their color	8 Sept.	Murayama
	(I) Did not check after setting (J) Holes numbers 1, 2 and 3 on insulation are hard to check (K) Attachment is in three different directions		5. (M), (N), (O), (P), (Q), (R), (S), (T)—Make trollies with separate compartments for checked and unchecked items	8 Sept.	Kamida
	(L) Hard to see in direct sunlight		Label compartments for checked items	8 Sept.	Murayama
	(M) No specified checking procedure (N) Trolley is packed full with cables alone (O) Cables placed on trolley are crossed over each other (P) Checked and unchecked items hard to tell apart	Systematic recurrence prevention measures	A System (operating division level, division level, department level, section level, etc.) B Technical standards (product standards, design standards, manufacturing standards, materials standards, inspection standards, testing and measurement standards, etc.) C Control standards (operating division regulations, department regulations, section regulations, design standards, inspection standards, work standards, etc.)		
	(Q), (R), (S) and (T) as above (M), (N), (O) and (P)		D Organization (operating-division shifts, department and section shifts, group shifts, etc.) E Training (operating division level, division level, department level, section level, etc.)		
	—		Details of above (clarify 5 W's and 1 H) Provide trollies with visual indication of checked and unchecked items		

64   THE QC PROBLEM-SOLVING APPROACH

Attached data
Technical analysis report
Design change contact person
Production lot analysis
Other

Merchandise plan
(1) Insufficient understanding of quality required by customer (customer needs)
1 Required quality characteristics missing
2 Required quality characteristics unclear
3 Levels of required quality characteristics set too liberally
4 Setting of required quality characteristics inadequately evaluated

Product plan
(2) Inadequate setting of design quality characteristics (including substitute characteristics)
1 Design quality characteristics missing
2 Design quality characteristics unclear
3 Levels of design quality characteristics set too liberally
4 Setting of design quality characteristics not sufficiently well evaluated
(3) Inadequate deployment to design specifications
1 Effects on other materials and parts not sufficiently well understood
2 External loading conditions, environmental stresses, etc. not sufficiently well understood
3 Countermeasures against abnormal loads inadequate
4 Quality characteristics of materials and parts not sufficiently well understood
5 Quality characteristics of materials and parts not expressed clearly enough
6 Production process capacity not sufficiently well understood
7 Handling of quality data inadequate

(4) Inadequate deployment to process plan (inadequate instructions)
1 Expressions on design diagrams inadequate
2 Standards for descriptions on design diagrams inadequate
3 Methods of expressing design quality inadequate
(5) Insufficient evaluation of design quality
1 Practicability of quality characteristics and substitute characteristics not checked sufficiently thoroughly
2 Quality evaluation standards unclear
3 Technology for evaluating quality lacking
4 Required quality not checked sufficiently thoroughly
(6) Inadequate change control (including first products of run)
1 Procedural standards for effecting changes inadequate
2 Procedural standards for effecting changes not observed
3 Checks for startup management insufficient

Preparation for production
(7) Inadequate process plans
1 Quality levels to be controlled in the process unclear
2 QC process charts not prepared carefully enough
3 Work-related standards insufficiently thoroughly prepared
4 Process control systems insufficiently thoroughly evaluated
5 Methods of evaluating process control systems unclear
6 Follow-up of items pointed out during test runs inadequate

(8) Inadequate control of equipment, jigs and tools
1 Control and setting of equipment, jigs and tools inadequate
2 Control and setting of equipment jigs and tools inadequately maintained
3 Control and setting of equipment, jigs and tools defective

Production
(9) Inadequate management of purchasing and subcontracting
1 Supplier selection standards inadequate
2 Process capability of incoming inspection not sufficiently well understood
3 Quality control of incoming inspection inadequate
4 Guidance on quality control in incoming inspection inadequate
5 Quality assurance agreement for incoming inspection inadequate
6 Incoming inspection standards unclear
7 Incoming inspection results not processed adequately
8 Information on defective materials and parts detected during production process not processed adequately
(10) Inadequate startup management
1 Standards for designating startup management period inadequate
2 Evaluation on transition to full-scale production (including specified contract goods) inadequate
3 Follow-up of items pointed out on trasition to full-scale production (including specified contract goods) inadequate
4 Quality checks during startup management phase inadequate

Figure 3.21—*Continued*

The QC Viewpoint—Vital for QC-Type Problem Solving

(11) Inadequate process control 1 Process control systems inadequate 2 Work methods inadequately controlled (ignorance) 3 Contents of work standards unlcear 4 Directions missing from work standards 5 Items missing from checksheets 6 Contents of QC process charts unclear 7 Control items missing from QC process charts 8 Process capability insufficient (dispersion) 9 No work standards 10 No checksheets 11 Inadvertent errors (forgot, overlooked, mistook) (12) Inadequate inspection management 1 Inspection plan unclear 2 Inspection technology lacking 3 Measuring and test equipment not inspected thoroughly enough 4 Feedback of inspection results to relevant departments inadequate 5 Analysis of inspection results inadequate **Sales and Service** (13) Inadequate service system 1 Contents of catalogs, instruction manuals and other materials inadequate 2 Insufficient public relations and technical explanations given to customer 3 Insufficient instructions given at time of purchase 4 Customer desires not passed on properly	**Information** (14) Inadequate information processing system 1 Quality information does not flow in a timely manner 2 Feedback mechanisms inadequate 3 Mechanisms for passing on quality information inadequate	Division responsible Date prepared: .... Division manager responsible .... Department manager .... Prepared by: ....

THE QC PROBLEM-SOLVING APPROACH

It is significant that standardization is defined not merely as the activity of establishing standards but also as the twin activities of establishing and utilizing them. A more direct way of defining it might be as follows:

Standardization means setting standards for materials and working methods and putting them into effect.

In promoting standardization within a company, it is necessary to proceed systematically by developing medium- and long-range policies and forecasts, and establishing or revising the standardization system.

When preparing work standards, it is important to ensure:

1. That the work procedures are appropriate.
2. That the standards are expressed in specific, concrete terms.
3. That the priorities are clear.
4. That the standards are easily understood and make plentiful use of diagrams and charts.

We should strive to avoid the "I set standards, you obey them" dichotomy and try to get everybody working together to formulate and observe standards.

The following list of checkpoints may be useful for evaluating a company's standardization system.

Standardization checkpoints
1. Is the standardization system companywide?
2. Is the setting, revision, and abolition of standards encouraged?
3. Have official procedures been laid down for setting, revising, and abolishing standards?
4. Is accumulation of technology promoted?
5. Are standards being utilized?
6. Are standards up-to-date and capable of being put into practice?
7. Are standards clear and specific, and not susceptible to different interpretations by different people?
8. Are there any inconsistencies among related standards?
9. Are the standards capable of being observed?
10. Do the layout and format of the standards make them easy to use?

3.11.2 Case Study: Work Standards Specifying Key Points

Standards must be easy to use, convenient, and easy to get used to. Figure 3.22 shows a "One-Point Standard Sheet" used by individual workers on a production line to standardize the key points of their work. These sheets elaborate the work standards even further, clarifying the key points of each work element. Some of their features are:

1. The models to which they apply are clearly specified.
2. They use sketches to facilitate understanding.
3. They itemize the key work points concisely.
4. They record the values of important characteristics clearly.
5. They specify causes, not results.

In this workplace, activities for formulating, revising, and observing standards are being developed in accordance with the scheme shown in Figure 3.23.

Amendment	Reason	Date	Name
⚠2	Official Change	21, Dec., 89	Miyamoto
⚠1	Through contact with Defect Eradication Committee Chairman	19, Sep., 89	Hosotani

One-Point Standard Sheet

Category QA-193

Approved	Approved	Approved	Approved	Prepared by:
✓	✓	✓	✓	
Ikeda	Yanagiya	Miyamoto	Hosotani	

Date: 13, Feb., 88
No. SM-08-0001
Filing Code: T-15

Title

Control of Electrodes during Mount Assembly Process

Applicable Models

AQ, PQ

☑ Unit
☐ Separate part

Key Point and Standard

(1) Use an electrode with a diameter of 5 mm for the upper electrode and a pure manganese electrode with a diameter of 6 mm as the lower electrode.

(2) Attach a heater to the upper electrode. Set the temperature of the tip of the electrode to 400 ± 20 °C.

(3) Set the gap between the upper and lower electrodes to 7 mm using a jig. With welding machines where the gap cannot be set to 7 mm, use a block gauge to set the gap on the line.

(4) Smooth the electrode faces with abrasive paper

Sketch

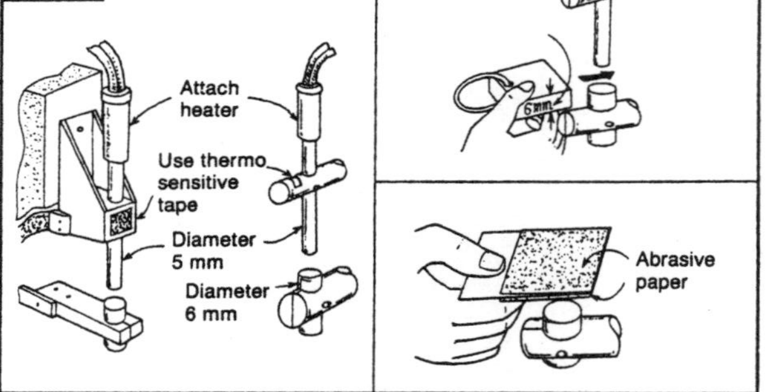

Attach heater
Use thermo sensitive tape
Diameter 5 mm
Diameter 6 mm
Abrasive paper

Inspection and Control Points

Do not use a diamond file on the electrode faces. Change the electrodes a minimum of 4 times per day at startup, 10:30, 12:45 and 15:00 (17:10). Change them more often when a large quantity of welding rod is used or welding takes place frequently.

Remarks

(1) The maximum length of the upper electrode is to be 200 mm.
(2) Use No. 600 abrasive paper (coarse) and finish off with No. 1,000 (fine).

Figure 3.22　Example of Work Standard Showing Key Points of Work

The QC Viewpoint—Vital for QC-Type Problem Solving 69

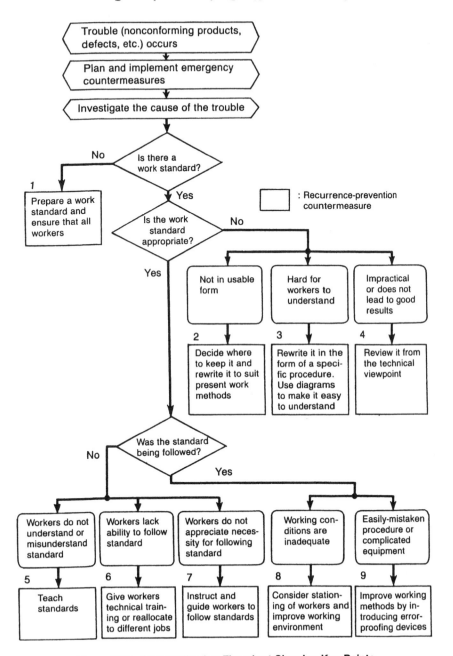

Figure 3.23 Standardization Flowchart Showing Key Points

CHAPTER 4

The QC Seven-Step Formula—Solving Problems the QC Way

Many sports and games have set plays and established tactics, and it is impossible to win without mastering these. Solving problems is exactly the same. No benefits will be achieved if the wrong procedure is followed or action is taken at random. If we want to improve our skill at devising more effective countermeasures—ones more likely to hit the mark—we have to know the correct way of going about it.

The QC Seven-Step Problem-Solving Formula (QC Seven-Step Formula for short) is the established strategy for solving problems in the workplace.

4.1 The Significance of the QC Seven-Step Formula
You can't get good without knowing the basics

The second of the three keys to solving problems the QC way is the QC Seven-Step Formula. As mentioned above, every sport or game has its own basic plays or strategies. We can enjoy taking part even without learning all these, but anyone who wants to become a Grand Master at chess or a single-figure player at golf must first become thoroughly conversant with the basics. You have probably met people at work who complain that their golf handicaps never seem to get any less. This is often because they are self-taught and have developed their own particular style of play without mastering the fundamentals.

Professor Jun'ichi Nishizawa of Tohoku University, a pioneer in the field of semiconductor engineering renowned worldwide for his development of devices such as static inductive transistors, semiconductor lasers, and optical fibers, has this to say about the importance of the basics[9]:

> In my case, I have rarely been successful because I happened to know something difficult. Success develops more often from the absolute basics. Some people boast about

72 THE QC PROBLEM-SOLVING APPROACH

how much they know, but knowing a lot is not such a big deal. It is more important
to understand the basics properly. It's enough just to know the simplest, most basic
things, for that is where the biggest opportunities for creativity lie. We don't have to
know anything very superior, we just have to understand the fundamentals well.

We can find many good problem solvers working in our companies: if
we observe the way they work, we see that they always stick to the basics.
In solving problems, this means following the QC Seven-Step Formula.

*The QC Seven-Step Formula is the basic procedure for solving problems
scientifically, rationally, efficiently, and effectively. It is a fundamental
problem-solving stratagem that allows any individual or group to solve even
difficult problems rationally and scientifically.*

If we want to achieve effective improvements more skillfully and accurately, we have to know the rules of the game—in other words, the QC
Seven-Step Formula. The secret of improving our problem-solving abilities
is to know this formula and act in accordance with it.

4.2   The QC Seven-Step Formula
Find and address the causes

The conventional method of solving problems is based on trial and error.
As illustrated in Figure 4.1, it consists of examining problems in the light
of experience, intuition, nerve or random inspiration, planning and implementing countermeasures based on this, and starting over again if things
do not go well. This approach, however, does not work with matters in which
we lack experience and will fail to solve the problem if our intuition is off
the mark.

Figure 4.1(2) contrasts this with the QC approach. The QC approach
to tackling problems can be split into three main stages, and the differences
between this and the conventional approach lie in stage 2. In the QC approach, we do not rely merely on experience and random inspiration, but
analyze the process based on factual data and accurately identify the factors adversely affecting the results (see Figure 4.2). We will never be able
to solve serious problems if we adopt countermeasures that just happen to
look good to us without identifying the true causes of the trouble.

In the QC approach, a standardized procedure has been established by
further subdividing the problem-solving process shown in Figure 4.1(2) into
seven steps, starting with "Select Topic" and finishing with "Standardize

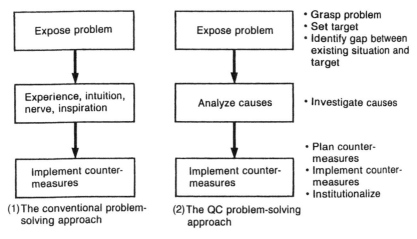

Figure 4.1 The Problem-Solving Process

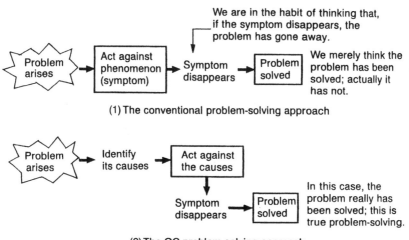

Figure 4.2 Problem-Solving Approaches

and Establish Control." This standardized procedure, illustrated in Table 4.1, is the QC Seven-Step Formula.

In the past, this formula has appeared in various guises, and QC literature and seminars have described a range of different steps for solving problems the QC way. Since different procedures are given even in the texts for seminars sponsored by the Union of Japanese Scientists and Engineers,

74 THE QC PROBLEM-SOLVING APPROACH

people have complained that it is difficult to establish a standard procedure throughout their company. The chairpersons (of which the author is one) and main committee members of the steering committees for JUSE's QC circle seminars (e.g., the QC Circle Instructor Course, the QC Circle Leader Course, and the QC Basic Course for Foremen) therefore met to discuss the problem and establish a standard version. The result is shown in Table 4.1.

Table 4.1 The QC 7-Step Problem-Solving Formula

Step No.	Basic Steps	Action Items
1	Select topic	• Identify problem • Decide topic
2	Understand Situation and Set Targets	Understand situation • Collect data • Decide characteristic to attack Set targets • Decide target (value and deadline)
3	Plan Activities	• Decide what to do • Decide schedule, division of responsibilities, etc.
4	Analyze Causes	• Check present values of characteristics • List possible causes • Analyze causes • Decide items to tackle
5	Consider and Implement Countermeasures	Consider countermeasures • Propose ideas for countermeasures • Discuss how to put countermeasures into effect • Check details of countermeasures Implement countermeasures • Plan how to implement countermeasures • Implement countermeasures
6	Check Results	• Check results of countermeasures • Compare results with targets • Identify tangible and intangible benefits
7	Standardize and Establish Control	Standardize • Establish new standards and revise old ones • Decide methods of control Establish control • Familiarize relevant people with new methods • Educate those responsible • Verify that benefits are being maintained

Note: Although the above basic order should be followed, it may be adjusted in some cases. For example, we may proceed from being given a target to understanding the situation, or we may select a topic after first understanding the situation.

The QC Seven-Step Formula—Solving Problems the QC Way   75

In the new QC Seven-Step Formula, the following points were clarified:

1. We decided to make Step 2, "Understand the Situation and Set Targets." This means analyzing data on the existing and past situations, deciding what to target, and setting target values.

2. We called Step 4, "Analyze Causes." Previously this step had titles such as "Analyze Status Quo," but we have renamed it in order to make its purpose more clear. The late Dr. Kaoru Ishikawa, the father of Japanese quality control, advised us that the phrase "Analyze Causes" was not right and that we should call this step "Analyze Process." In the Japanese construction industry, however, the word "process" means "the state of progress of the work"; and the word "process" is also not so acceptable to people in service industries. On the other hand, the phrase "Analyze Causes" is widely used. We therefore decided to use it in the sense of "analyze the process and identify the causes."

3. We made Step 7, "Standardize and Establish Control." In the past, this step was known by names such as "Apply the brakes," "Prevent backsliding," or "Effect a permanent fix." Although these phrases are very apt, they tend to be misunderstood as meaning standardization alone, and the sense of establishing control is easily missed. Failing to check the effect of countermeasures is like omitting the finishing touches to a painting. We therefore renamed this step to prevent this.

This is how the new version of the old QC problem-solving procedure was developed. To ensure that our problem-solving activities proceed as rationally, effectively, and efficiently as possible, it is vital to follow this formula faithfully, step by step. Doing so will enable us to solve even the trickiest problems and achieve superb results. The next section describes each of the seven steps in the formula in more detail.

4.3   Putting the QC Seven-Step Formula into Practice
Move forward one step at a time

Step 1: Select Topic
The first step in problem solving is to find a problem and decide on the topic to be addressed. Since everybody will then work together on the project for the next three to six months, it is important to select a challenging and motivating topic.

We might think that problems are easy to find as long as people are problem-conscious, but this is not the case. We must be problem-conscious, but we also need a technique for selecting topics. Such a technique is described below.

Substep 1: Check the roles of one's division, department, and job. Each division and department within a company has its own particular role to play and function to perform. We must start by understanding how we should perform our work and how our workplace should be set up. To establish the role and function of a division or department, we will probably need to take a fresh look at documents such as work allocation regulations and divisional and departmental function deployment charts.

Substep 2: Check the policies and objectives assigned to the workplace. It is desirable for the topics we select to reflect higher-level policies. We should re-read our division manager's annual policy statement and our section manager's annual implementation plans, and recheck the issues we are required to address during the current financial period. We should then reflect on whether or not we are adequately fulfilling our role in implementing these annual policies.

Substep 3: Identify and list problems. Using the approaches shown in Figure 4.3, identify problems by examining divisional and departmental roles, division and section managers' policies, day-to-day problems, requests from superiors, QC circle annual activity plans, and so on, and organize

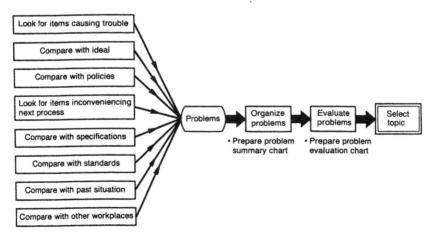

Figure 4.3 Approaches to Identifying Problems

them in the form of a "topic chart." It is a good idea to pursue the identification of problems from the following two perspectives:

- What kind of problems are giving us trouble?
- What things would we like to improve further?

Substep 4: Evaluate the problems and select a topic. Select one important topic from among the problems listed in substep 3. Sometimes the circle members can easily decide on the topic by discussion. In other cases a "problem evaluation chart" such as that shown in Table 4.2 should be used to single one out. We should also remember to have our superiors evaluate the topics and give their opinions.

A good way of expressing a topic is as follows:

Describing a topic

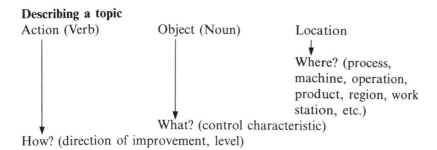

Examples of topics

- Reduce welding defects in automobile assembly process.
- Reduce setup time of dialyzer.
- Improve bending accuracy in process for manufacturing guttering.
- Increase number of shopping-club cards issued in Kinki region.

Seven points to note about describing topics:

1. State where the improvement is to take place (name of process, title of job, name of product, etc.).
2. Make it obvious from the title of the topic what is to be done and what the objective is.
3. Express the topic in terms of attacking something bad rather than improving something good (this is because the latter style of expression tends to lead people to chase after the ideal and rely too much on the help of others):

Table 4.2   Problem Evaluation Chart

Item	Suitability for Circle					Need for Improvement				Score	Order of priority
Evaluation criteria	Is the problem common to all circle members? • Common to all members • Common to most members • Only relevant to a few members	How easy is it for the members to tackle the problem as a circle? • Highly relevant problem of great interest • Topic too ambitious • Too much affected by others outside circle	Will the members be able to cooperate together? • No worries on this score • Yes, with a little effort • Not satisfactorily	How long will the project take? • 3-5 months • 2 months or less • 6 months or more	Will it help to raise the circle's abilities? • Difficult problem but will raise abilities • Will raise abilities if effort is made • Just a casual idea	How great is the need for improvement? • Requires urgent attention • Important but not very urgent • Not urgent	Does it meet workplace needs? • Is inconveniencing others • Must be dealt with now • Not very relevant	How much will the activities cost? • Will incur no extra costs • Minor costs only • Expensive	What sorts of results can be expected? • Reward in proportion to effort • Fairly good results • Minor results only		
Maximum scores	5	5	5	5	5	7	5	5	8	50	
Eliminate grinding cracks	5	5	5	5	5	7	3	5	8	48	1
Improve efficiency of hole pitch process	5	3	3	5	5	7	5	5	8	46	2
Improve safety and hygiene scores	3	3	5	3	3	5	1	5	2	30	5
Introduce computer processing	1	1	3	1	5	2	1	1	5	20	8
Reduce assembly labor-hours	5	5	5	1	5	5	3	5	8	42	3

Note: Figures in brackets against evaluation criteria indicate scores.

The QC Seven-Step Formula—Solving Problems the QC Way　79

- Improve good-product rate→reduce defect rate.
- Improve delivery→reduce number of days late.

4. Express in terms of results rather than methods:

   - Standardize fixtures and fittings for hotel guest rooms→reduce number of missed fixtures and fittings in hotel guest rooms.
   - Prepare instruction manual for hotel reservation calls→reduce time callers are kept waiting when reserving rooms by telephone.

5. Do not confuse countermeasures with topics:

   - Improve product education for sales staff→improve sales staff's product knowledge.
   - Improve torque-fastening method→decrease torque-fastening defect rate.

6. Express in clear, commanding terms:

   - Let's reduce the defect rate→reduce defect rate.

7. If necessary, append subtopics. Do this when you wish to emphasize a special characteristic of the problem-solving activity or the uniqueness of a countermeasure. In these examples, the subtopic follows the dash after the topic:

   - Reduce changeover time—solve difficult problems by having people speak with facts.
   - Reduce repair time for noncontact relay grinders—creativity, ingenuity, and study for mastering use of new machines.
   - Reduce number of reversed joints—a tale of hardship in QC circle activities by part-timers.

Well-chosen topics satisfy the following five conditions:

1. Common to all circle members.
2. Highly necessary and relevant to one's job.
3. Challenging but achievable.
4. Linked to divisional and departmental policies and objectives.
5. Able to raise the ability levels of the circle or group.

80   THE QC PROBLEM-SOLVING APPROACH

Case study

When addressing problems, what specifically must we do in order to follow the QC Seven-Step Formula? Let's look at the problem-solving process by means of an example.

For this case study, I have selected the following topic taken up by the "Second Circle" at Chigasaki Plant, Toto Ltd.:

Reduce the Defect Rate in the Plastic Bathtub Manufacturing Process[10c]

The "Second Circle" was formed in June 1969 and consists of two men and two women with an average age of thirty-seven. Its catch-phrase is "self-management" and it liaises with other processes to solve problems and evolve its activities through continuous study.

1. *Introduction.*   Our workplace is Chigasaki Plant, Toto Ltd. in the eastern part of Chigasaki, home of the Hamaori Festival. The factory makes sanitary ware, plastic bathtubs, modular bathrooms, and new ceramics products. We belong to the No. 2 Group in the Plastics Production Department and are responsible for the production process for artificial marble bathtubs. We tackle our manufacturing work by emphasizing the hands-on approach and close liaison with other processes, and our aim is to eliminate in-process defects.

2. *Outline of process.*   The bath manufacturing process consists of nine subprocesses with five quality circles. We are responsible for the "reinforcing process." Figure 4.4 shows an outline of the manufacturing process.

3. *Reason for selecting topic.*   We are working on projects originally planned at the beginning of 1987, but the defect rate has tended to increase recently, and our department has not achieved its targets. Based on requests from our superior, we have therefore decided to tackle the topic titled "Reduce the Defect Rate in the Plastic Bathtub Manufacturing Process."

The QC Seven-Step Formula—Solving Problems the QC Way   81

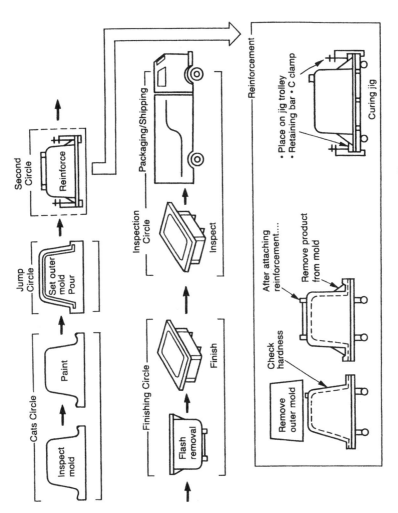

Figure 4.4 The Bathtub Manufacturing Process

82　THE QC PROBLEM-SOLVING APPROACH

Comment
The most important thing in formulating problems is to be problem-conscious. The first step is to raise the awareness of problems on the part of circle members, bring hidden problems to light, and make the need for improvement painfully obvious. The "Second Circle" noticed that the defect rate in plastic bathtubs had increased lately, and they immediately took this up as their topic. When a problem is noticed, it is important not to ignore it but to break out of the situation by tackling the problem right away.

Step 2: Understand Situation and Set Targets
Investigate the present situation in regard to the topic selected, and set targets.

Substep 1: Decide on the characteristic to be addressed.　In this substep, we decide what control characteristics to tackle. The control characteristics selected at this stage will also be used later to measure how effective the countermeasures have been in achieving the objectives. Table 4.3 shows some typical control characteristics[2].

Substep 2: Understand the situation.　Survey the past trends and present situation in order to identify the existing levels of the control characteristics selected in substep 1 and the form in which the deficiencies are appearing.

The term "situation" here means not just the situation at the present time but the overall situation extending from past to present. "Understand the situation" means finding out how bad things are now and what they were like in the past. We therefore investigate at this stage how the control characteristics have changed with time.

In understanding the situation, we should be aware of the following seven key points:

1. Check past data concerning the characteristic values and collect fresh data to ensure that the problem can be expressed numerically.
2. Investigate the flow of work and the state of the process.
3. Examine the situation over a period of time and find out what sorts of changes have occurred.
4. Ferret out problems by stratifying the data (by place, person, machine, method, etc.).
5. Pay attention to dispersion and deviation.
6. Be priority-oriented and narrow down the priorities.
7. Utilize the Seven QC Tools.

The QC Seven-Step Formula—Solving Problems the QC Way 83

Table 4.3 Examples of Control Characteristics

Target	Characteristic	Application
Quality	Number of defects	Reducing annealing strength defects in steel plate, etc.
	Number of mistakes	Reducing mistakes in preparing invoices, attaching parts, etc.
	Number of reworked items	Reducing number of defects reworked
	Weight	Controlling weights of tablets, parts, etc.
	Time	Controlling work times, processing times, etc.
	Thickness	Controlling plate thicknesses, parts dimensions, etc.
	Number of error-proofing devices	Reducing human error
	Power consumption, current, load voltage	Controlling central values and dispersion of electrical characteristics
	Defect rate	Reducing number of processing defects and defective final products
Cost	Yield	Controlling output of tablets and other products
	Consumption	Reducing consumption of electrical power, consumables, water, etc.
	Inventory	Controlling stocks of consumables and merchandise
	Energy consumption	Improving energy-saving, reducing heavy-oil consumption per product unit
	Personnel costs and other overheads	Cost control
	Labor-hours	Reducing labor-hours
	Budget/spending ratio	Reducing manufacturing costs
	Materials costs	Rreducing costs of resins, insulating materials, etc.
Productivity	Production output per unit time	Controlling production volume
	Process time	Increasing daily production volume
	Lead time	Reducing time taken from receipt of raw materials to output of product
	Yield	Increasing yield of steel plate, etc.
	Sales	Increasing sales volume per person
	Availability	Reducing equipment downtime
	Idle time	Reducing idle time for input and output media
Efficiency	Work efficiency	Decreasing actual work times and standard times
	Changeover time	Reducing equipment changeover times
	Inspection time	Reducing inspection labor-hours
	Setup times	Eliminating waste from setups
	Transportation time	Reducing transportation time
	Administration time	Improving efficiency of ordering, transcribing, etc.
	Job (computation) execution time	Reducing number of program steps per unit time

THE QC PROBLEM-SOLVING APPROACH

Table 4.3—Continued

Target	Characteristic	Application
Delivery	Compliance rate	Improve delivery compliance rate (average days late per unit delivered)
	Total days late	Improve on-time shipping rate (ratio of items shipped on time to total items shipped) for different models
	On-time delivery rate	Improve on-time delivery rate (ratio of items delivered on time to total items delivered)
	Inspection holdups	Eliminate delivery problems due to late inspections
	Lot-out number	Reduce number of rejected lots
	Output	Control daily output
	Lead times	Shorten lead times
	Process delays	Reduce number of process delays
Sales	Number of units sold	Monitoring degree of achievement of sales targets
	Sales amounts	Checking budget achievement rate
	Profit and loss	Improving profitability
	Number of sales visits	Increase number of sales visits to retail outlets
	Added value	Controlling profit
Safety	Number of sudden realizations and cold shivers	Preventing accidents at work
	Number of danger anticipation training courses	Enhancing safety training
	Number of accident-free days	Improving safety consciousness
	Effluent water BOD (biological oxygen demand) compliance rate	Cleaning up the environment and preventing pollution
	Accident severity rate	Comparing with previous years, raising safety consciousness
	Accident frequency rate	Accident statistics
	Seat belt wearing rate	Preventing road injuries
	Number of unsafe items reported by safety patrols	Eliminating unsafe places
Human relations	Attendance rate	Monitoring attendance
	Number of suggestions	Energizing the workplace and promoting improvement suggestion schemes
	Number of morning meetings	Familiarizing with higher-level policies
	Meeting attendance rate	Improving awareness of activities
	Rate of participation in recreational activities	Creating vigorous workplaces
	Number of workplace discussion meetings	Bolstering workplace communication
QC circles	Meeting participation rate	Improving participation in meetings
	QC tool utilization rate	Raising circle's abilities
	Number of topics completed	Increasing number of topics completed
	Number of activity reports submitted	Identifying state of activities of circles

The QC Seven-Step Formula—Solving Problems the QC Way   85

Table 4.3—*Continued*

Target	Characteristic	Application
QC circles	Number of topics presented Annual financial benefits Number of meetings Number of suggestions Circle activity evaluation score	Keeping circles alive Raising level of activities Promoting circle activities Raising morale Raising circle's abilities
Service	Number of complaints Time taken to transfer telephone calls Telephone waiting time Immediate-response rate Time taken to deal with abnormalities Repair times	Preventing recurrence of complaints and improving service Reducing time taken per call for call transfer Reducing waiting time for outside callers Improving rate of immediate responses to inquiries Controlling provisional and permanent countermeasures Reducing times taken to repair office equipment

Substep 3: Decide on targets and the time limits for their achievement. A target is a number indicating the level of improvement that must be attained. It is determined by balancing the ideal against restrictions such as time constraints and the amount·of manpower and money available for investment in the project.

Do not set vague objectives such as "We would like to stop giving the wrong change at the cash registers," or "We would like to raise the recovery rate of accounts receivable."

Targets must clarify the following three points:

1. What? (control characteristic)—e.g., value of mistaken change.
2. By when? (time limit)—e.g., by November.
3. By how much? (target value)—e.g., reduce from $500/month to $50/month.

To answer the question "What?" we first decide what we want to do in the current round of improvements, confirm this by examining the topic closely, and then decide what to set as the target in light of the topic's improvement objective. "By when?" means the date by which the topic is to be concluded. A topic is concluded when we have implemented countermeasures, standardized our methods, and made sure that the benefits are being maintained. "By how much?" means a specific value for the degree of improvement to be achieved by the project.

86   THE QC PROBLEM-SOLVING APPROACH

Since targets are the goals of our problem-solving activities, they must be expressed in concrete, easily understood terms. We should already have grasped the existing level of performance in relation to the control characteristics in Step 2, "Understand the Situation." The target values we set will therefore depend on the degree of difficulty of the topic and the problem-solving abilities of the group.

There are no fixed rules for deciding on target values, but they are usually chosen from considerations such as the following:

1. The amount by which we want to reduce the number of defects or nonconforming products.
2. By comparison with values set by other divisions.
3. Values that must logically be so.
4. Values that must be achieved regardless of other considerations (e.g., those relating to safety and pollution prevention).

The following are some standard target-setting approaches:

- The zero approach—reduce the number of defects or nonconforming products to zero.
- The halving approach—halve the number of defects or nonconforming products.
- The one-third approach—reduce the number of defects or nonconforming products to a third of their present values.

The seven conditions that well-set targets must satisfy are as follows:

1. They must produce benefits that outweigh the cost and effort of producing them.
2. They must be high enough to provide motivation.
3. They must be capable of being achieved.
4. It must be possible to check whether or not they have been achieved.
5. All involved must accept them and believe in them.
6. They must stimulate desire and action on the part of the group members.
7. Their relevance to higher-level policies and other departments must have been carefully considered.

Case study (*continued*)
   4. Understand the situation.   Based on the high defect rate of December 1986, we stratified and analyzed the data as shown in Figure 4.5

The QC Seven-Step Formula—Solving Problems the QC Way

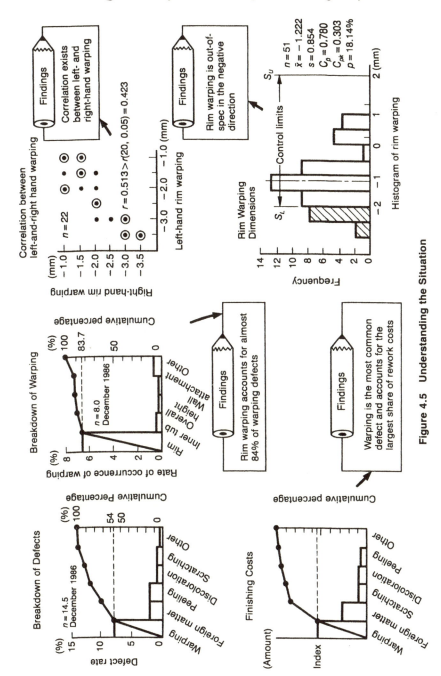

Figure 4.5 Understanding the Situation

and discovered that the rate of rim-warping defects (dimensions of long sides of rim lying outside the specification limits) was the highest, that there was a correlation between left- and right-hand warping, and that the deviation from the control limits ($\pm$ 2 mm) was 18 percent in the negative direction.

5. *Set targets.* The target values were set as shown in Figure 4.6 with a view to achieving the departmental objectives by reducing the defect rate, also bearing in mind the targets for QC circle effort.

Figure 4.6 Setting a Target

Comment

The aim of this step is to expose what has been wrong up to now and to orient the activities by deciding what to tackle and how to proceed. If this step is not taken properly, the subsequent steps will run into a blind alley.

In this example, the data were analyzed using Pareto charts and the problem was narrowed down to "rim warping" by prioritizing. Histograms also showed that the process capability was insufficient. The circle has used QC tools skillfully to identify the shortcomings of the existing setup.

Step 3: Plan Activities

In this step, we prepare a plan designed to ensure that our problem-solving activities go smoothly. We do this by answering the questions "Who?" and "How?" In other words, we draw up a plan for working together on the project, and allocate people's responsibilities.

The QC Seven-Step Formula—Solving Problems the QC Way 89

Substep 1: Decide action items. Here, we decide on the action items: that is, we decide how to proceed with investigating the existing situation, analyzing the causes, and so on, in accordance with the QC Seven-Step Formula. Next, we assign responsibilities for each of these items, taking account of the situation in the workplace and the individual abilities of the circle members. Responsibilities should be shared out in such a way as to draw on the members' particular specializations and talents. Every member must be willing to undertake his or her fair share of the work so that it does not fall on the shoulders of a few.

Substep 2: Decide schedule of activities. Discuss when each of the action items should be started and by when it should be completed, and decide on a schedule. The project should generally last for about three to four months. This is because activities like this inevitably tend to run out of steam if allowed to go on longer, and the project will grind to a halt.

It is best to allocate responsibility for all the action items, but this is sometimes impossible or difficult to decide at this stage. In such cases, responsibility should be allocated broadly and broken down into more detail as the project proceeds.

Substep 3: Draw up an activity plan. In this step, an activity plan like that shown in Table 4.4 is drawn up in the form of a bar chart, arrow diagram, and the like.

Table 4.4 Plan of Problem-Solving Activities

Circle name: La Traviata Circle   Date prepared: 21 March

No.	Action Item	Leader	April	May	June	July	August
1	Select Topic	Ikeda	▬				
2	Understand Situation and Set Targets	Hino	▬				
3	Plan Activities	Ikeda		▬			
4	Analyze Causes	Hino, Matsubara			▬▬		
5	Consider and Implement Countermeasures	Matsubara				▬	
6	Check Results	Matsubara				▬	
7	Standardize and Establish Control	Takigawa					▬

Note: ▬▬ Planned, ---- Actual

90 THE QC PROBLEM-SOLVING APPROACH

Table 4.5 Activity Plan

One Role per Person—Striving for Self Management   - - - - - Planned —— Actual

Why?	What?	Who?	By when?				How?	Reflections on previous activities; present method of attack
Objective	Activity step	Step leader	1987 Jan.	Feb.	Mar.	Apr.	Tool	
Check the facts	Understand Situation	Kojima	- - - → ⟶				Stratification, Pareto diagrams	Better inter-process liaison and more extensive use of QC tools
Why have things gone wrong?	Analyze Causes	Sugimoto	- - - - - → ⟶				Scatter diagrams, etc.	
What should be done?	Consider and Implement Countermeasures	Tamegai		- - - → ⟶			Relations diagrams, etc.	
Can improvement be sustained?	Check Results	Onoda			- - → ⟶		Pareto diagrams, etc.	
Standardize and Establish Control	Applying the brakes	Ono				- - → ⟶	Graphs and standards	
	Reflections and future approaches	Ohara				- → ⟶	Brainstorming sessions, etc.	

Target: QC Circle Promotion Office activity score of 70 points or more   14 January 1986

Comment

The "Second Circle" members have thoroughly discussed their previous round of activities and the problems they had with operating the circle, and they have incorporated the findings of their review into the current activity plan. They have done a splendid job in rotating the PDCA Wheel with regard to their QC circle activities.

They have also chosen to appoint a different leader for each step of the QC Seven-Step Formula to ensure that everybody participates fully, and this is also an excellent idea.

When preparing activity plans, a good method is to ask ourselves the 5 Ws and 1 H and incorporate the answers into the plan, as shown in Table 4.5.

Step 4: Analyze Causes

Once the targets have been decided and the activity plan has been drawn up, the next step is to analyze the causes. This is the most important step in the formula.

Accurately identifying the true causes tells us what to do in the next step: considering and implementing countermeasures. If we do not clearly iden-

The QC Seven-Step Formula—Solving Problems the QC Way   91

tify the causes, we are likely to waste time and money trying out various ineffective schemes.

Analyzing the causes means using QC tools to investigate the relationship between causes and quality characteristics and pinpointing the particular factors that are adversely affecting the characteristics. Here, "causes" means the main factors that are creating problems and appear likely to be influencing the results of the process.

The purpose of analyzing the causes is to find out what measures should be taken against what factors. If the cause-and-effect relationships are not accurately identified at this stage, we will end up saying such things as, "We took action but nothing improved," or "We didn't get any benefit."

The causes should be analyzed according to the procedure entailed in the following substeps:

Substep 1: Summarize the system of characteristics and causes on a cause-and-effect diagram. Start by listing the various possible causes. Hold a brainstorming session attended by all those directly and indirectly involved in the work, gather large numbers of opinions, and draw up a cause-and-effect diagram. Causes should be expressed in terms of what is wrong with the present situation, for example, "tile strength is low" or "taking out documents is time-consuming."

Next, examine all the possible causes entered on the cause-and-effect diagram on the basis of technical knowledge and experience, and single out those considered to have a particularly strong effect—the ones that ought to be checked by collecting data. Highlight these on the diagram.

Substep 2: Analyze the relationships between characteristics and causes using QC tools. In this step, we examine what we consider to be the most important causes on the cause-and-effect diagram to find out which are the true ones and what relationship they bear to the characteristics. The important thing here is not to guess but to identify the facts correctly. To do this, we should analyze data such as the following using QC tools:

1. Past data.
2. Stratified daily data.
3. Fresh data obtained from experiments in the workplace.

When analyzing data, we should remember to do the following:

1. Examine differences between strata. Stratify the data according to the 4 Ms (Machines, Manpower, Materials, and Methods), prepare

92 THE QC PROBLEM-SOLVING APPROACH

stratified graphs, histograms, scatter diagrams, and control charts, and look to see whether or not there are any differences between different strata.

2. Examine time changes. Use graphs, checksheets, and control charts to see whether or not the characteristics and causes are changing with time.

3. Investigate correlation. Prepare scatter diagrams and check for correlation between paired sets of data—that is, between causes and characteristics, causes and causes, and characteristics and characteristics.

4. Investigate the workplace and the hardware. Carefully observe the workplace and the people and things in it. If complaints have been made about nonconforming items or products, use equipment such as electron microscopes if needed.

Substep 3: Summarize the results of the analysis. Draw conclusions by applying technical considerations to the statistical results obtained.

Substep 4: Decide what items to tackle. Decide on the items against which countermeasures must be instituted.

Case Study (*continued*)

7. *Analyze causes.* We prepared a cause-and-effect diagram for the rim warping. From this, we extracted four main factors and used a points system to decide the order in which they should be checked (see Figure 4.7).

a. "Personal differences." There was variation in the tightening of the C clamps because these were tightened by hand. When the torque was checked, it was found to be generally lower than the desired value. It was also clear that a lower torque increased the likelihood of the rim warping exceeding the control limits.

b. "Hardness." The hardness of the plastic used for the bathtubs satisfied the standard on the process capability chart. When the change in rim warping for various hardnesses was checked, there was found to be no correlation at the 5 percent significance level.

c. "Deformation." There was strong positive correlation between the warping of the retaining bars and the number of times they had been used, and strong negative correlation between the number of times the retaining bars had been used and the rim warping.

d. "Warping." The curing jigs were bowed in the negative direction. When the correlation between the bowing of the curing jigs and

The QC Seven-Step Formula—Solving Problems the QC Way   93

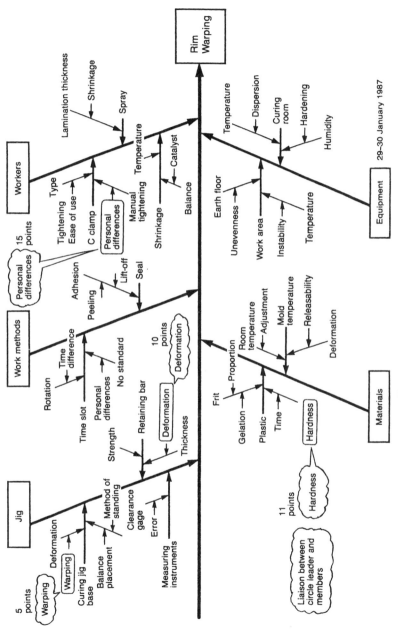

Figure 4.7 Analysis of Causes

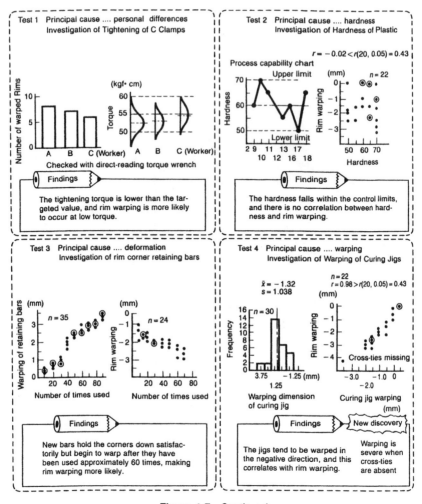

Figure 4.7—*Continued*

the rim warping was checked, there was found to be a positive correlation at the 5 percent significance level.

A new fact was also discovered: missing cross-ties on the curing-jig trolleys was also a cause of rim warping.

Comment
It is important to check whether the causes highlighted on the cause-and-

The QC Seven-Step Formula—Solving Problems the QC Way   95

effect diagram are in fact the true causes. In other case studies we often see causes taken from the cause-and-effect diagram and immediately subjected to countermeasures without being investigated to see whether they are in fact the true causes. This approach is risky, because the causes listed on cause-and-effect diagrams often consist of random guesses or preconceived ideas on the part of the circle members, and may not represent the true facts.

The "Second Circle" collected facts and data on four factors: personal differences, hardness, deformation, and warping, and checked these using QC tools. The way they have analyzed the causes, using scatter diagrams to determine the relationship between causes and effects, and histograms to check the degree of dispersion, is excellent. The fact that they have used the Seven QC Tools appropriately shows that this circle has studied diligently and is operating at a high level.

Step 5: Consider and Implement Countermeasures

In this step, we think up strategies for eliminating the true causes pinpointed by our analysis, and then put these strategies into effect. To find out what kind of countermeasures will be effective in eliminating the causes, we pool the ideas of the circle members, evaluate these ideas, and draw up action plans.

Substep 1: Propose ideas for countermeasures.   In this step, we think up as many possible countermeasures as we can, paying attention to the following points:

- Consider the problem from all angles.
- Collect ideas from superiors and people in upstream and downstream processes as well.
- Do not judge the ideas at the creation stage.
- Use lateral thinking.

To collect a wide range of ideas, it is best to use knowledge-pooling techniques such as brainstorming or the affinity diagram method (one of the Seven New QC Tools). Other effective methods for eliciting ideas include "idea-generating strategies," defect listing, requirements listing, characteristics listing, and the question-and-answer method (the checklist method). Some idea-generating strategies are given in Table 4.6, and three question-and-answer techniques—the 4M technique, the 5W1H technique, and the WUS (waste, unevenness, and strain) technique—are shown in Tables 4.7, 4.8, and 4.9.

96　THE QC PROBLEM-SOLVING APPROACH

Table 4.6　Idea-Generating Strategies

Strategy	Key Point	Example
1. Elimination	What would happen if we did away with this?	Replace milk bottles by cardboard cartons (eliminating collection of empties)
2. Reversal	What would happen if we did the opposite?	Replace static blood-donor centers with mobile vans (bring things to people instead of having people go to things — i.e. do things the opposite way round)
3. Normal and exceptional	Is this unusual, or does it happen all the time?	Abolish timecards, monitor late arrivals and overtime only (control abnormal situation only)
4. Constant and variable	What would happen if we only controlled the things that change?	Divide dining-hall menu into set menu and a la carte (control exceptions)
5. Expansion and contraction	What would happen if we made this bigger or smaller?	Portable televisions and cassette recorders (decrease size to make transportation easier)
6. Combination and separation	What would happen if we combined or separated these?	Combine hammer and nail puller (combine functions)
7. Collection and dispersion	Try bringing things together or placing them apart	Combine telephone with answering machine, use trailers for storage (streamlining)
8. Addition and subtraction	Try adding something or taking it away	Combine broom, brush and dustpan — vacuum cleaner (integrate functions)
9. Changing order	Try assembling in a different order or changing the work sequence	Keep out of debt by earning money before spending it rather than buying now and paying later
10. Same and different	Try making use of differences	Use bolts of different color or shape for error-proofing (highlight differences)
11. Sufficiency and substitution	Can it be used for some other purpose? Can it be replaced by something else?	Remove material from old umbrella and use frame to dry rags on (re-use of scrap)
12. Parallel and series	Try doing things simultaneously or one after another	Use a blind brush to dust several slats of a venetian blind at once (arranging tasks in parallel)

The QC Seven-Step Formula—Solving Problems the QC Way   97

Table 4.7   The 4M Technique

① Manpower	• Are workers observing the standards? • Are they working efficiently? • Are they problem-conscious? • Do they have a strong sense of responsibility? • Are they skilled? • Are they experienced? • Are they assigned to the right jobs? • Do they want to improve? • Are human relations good? • Are they healthy?	③ Machines	• Is the quantity right? • Is the grade right? • Is the brand right? • Are they free of impurities? • Are they stocked in the right quantities? • Are they being used without waste? • Are they being handled correctly? • Are any materials-in-process left lying around? • Are they properly distributed? • Are their quality levels satisfactory? • Are they appropriately laid out? • Are there too many or too few? • Are they tidy and well-organized?
② Materials	• Do they meet production requirements? • Do they meet process capabilities? • Are they being properly lubricated? • Are they being thoroughly inspected? • Are they free of breakdowns and stoppages? • Are they sufficiently precise? • Are they free of abnormal noise?	④ Methods	• Are work standards satisfactory? • Are work standards kept up to date? • Are the methods safe? • Do the methods ensure good products? • Are the methods efficient? • Is the work sequence appropriate? • Is changeover satisfactory? • Are temperatures and humidities appropriate? • Is lighting and ventilation adequate? • Is there good liaison between previous and subsequent processes?

Table 4.8   The 5W1H Technique

① Who?	• Who is to do it? • Who is doing it? • Who should be doing it? • Who else could do it? • Who else should do it? • Who is allowing WUS (waste, unevenness and strain) to occur?	④ When?	• Where is it to be done? • Where is it being done? • Where should it be done? • Where else could it be done? • Where else should it be done? • Where is WUS occurring?
② What?	• When is it to be done? • When is it being done? • When should it be done? • When else could it be done? • When else should it be done? • When is WUS occurring?	⑤ Where?	• Why is that person to do it? • Why do it? • Why do it there? • Why do it then? • Why do it that way? • Is any WUS occurring in our thinking?
③ Why?	• What is to be done? • What is being done? • What should be done? • What else could be done? • What else should be done? • What WUS is occurring?	⑥ How?	• How is it to be done? • How is it being done? • How should it be done? • How else could it be done? • How else should it be done? • Is any WUS caused by the method?

98   THE QC PROBLEM-SOLVING APPROACH

Table 4.9   The WUS (Waste, Unevenness and Strain) Technique

Manpower	Waste	• Is the number of workers appropriate for the amount of work? • Is there an excessive amount of time-on-hand? • Are the right materials in the right place at the right time? • Is there any wasteful motion? • Is there any waste in the way work is allocated? • Is there any waste due to poor planning or setting up?
	Unevenness	• Are people in one area rushed off their feet while those in other areas have nothing to do? • Is the mix of experienced and inexperienced workers right? • Are people too busy at one time and too idle at others? • Is there any unevenness in the provision of training and instruction?
	Strain	• Are there enough people to cope with the workload? • Is any work being done manually that ought to be done by machines? • Are people getting over-tired through working in strained postures?
Materials	Waste	• Are yields too low? • Are still-usable items being thrown away? • Are expensive materials being used where cheaper ones would suffice? • Are too many defective products being produced? • Is unnecessary rework being done because of poor organization of materials? • Is corrosion being effectively prevented? • Are supplementary materials being wasted? • Is electric power being wasted? • Is there any waste due to poor design?
	Unevenness	• Are materials, parts, etc of uniform quality? • Is there any irregularity in the properties of materials? • Are products unevenly finished?
	Strain	• Is the strength sufficient for safety? • Is there any strain in outsourced items (delivery requirements, quality?) • Is there any strain due to poor design?
Machines	Waste	• Are machines being under-utilized? • Are machines and tools being used effectively? • Is there any waste due to poor layout of equipment? • Are any machines lying idle?
	Unevenness	• Are the production capacities of the various machines balanced? • Is equipment being used unreasonably or wastefully?
	Strain	• Are equipment lifetimes being shortened by using them over their designed capacity? • Is equipment being looked after sufficiently well? • Is low-precision equipment being asked to perform high-precision processing?

Substep 2: Select countermeasure proposals.   Evaluate the countermeasure proposals put forward in the previous substep from the following viewpoints, and select the ones that appear effective and feasible:

The QC Seven-Step Formula—Solving Problems the QC Way

1. Effect—Does it seem likely to crack the problem effectively?
2. Feasibility—Is it technically possible?
3. Economy—How expensive is it to implement?

Substep 3: Discuss how to put the countermeasures into effect. Once a countermeasure has been selected, the next step is to consider how to implement it. Answering the 5Ws and 1 H is a good way to approach this.

While the circle members must confirm the countermeasure plans among themselves, they should also report to their superiors and receive their approval.

Substep 4: Implement countermeasures. Carefully consider how each countermeasure is to be implemented, prepare provisional production standards and provisional work standards, and implement the countermeasure in accordance with these standards.

Case Study (*continued*)

8. *Consider and implement countermeasures.* A systematic diagram was used to summarize the countermeasures based on the facts determined from the investigations performed in the previous step, an action plan was prepared, and the three items with a priority ranking of 1 were implemented, as shown in Figure 4.8.

Comment

The countermeasures proposed for eliminating the rim warping were skillfully narrowed down by having all the circle members evaluate them in terms of their feasibility and predicted benefits. The optimum conditions for each of these proposals were then identified and quantified.

The expected results, however, are not always achieved, even when the countermeasure proposals are carefully thought out. The "Second Circle" therefore performed experiments and did trial fabrications, collecting and analyzing fresh data to determine whether or not each countermeasure was in fact producing the desired results. This really is the right way to go about it. A further strength of this particular circle is the way in which they look very closely at the workplace and the actual people and things in it.

100   THE QC PROBLEM-SOLVING APPROACH

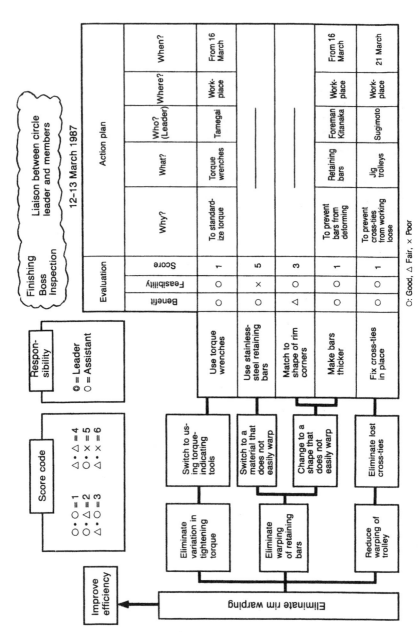

Figure 4.8 Countermeasure Plan and Implementation

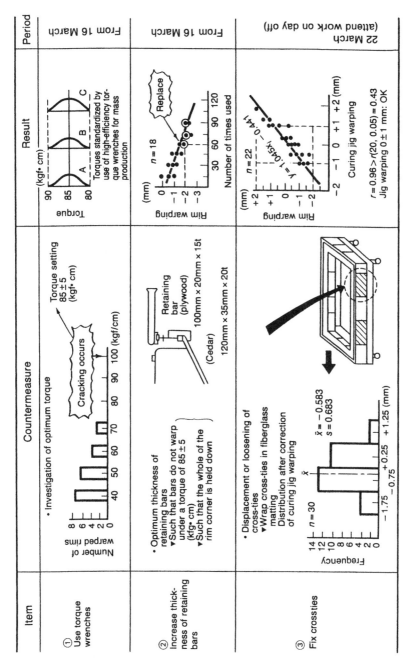

Figure 4.8—Continued

102   THE QC PROBLEM-SOLVING APPROACH

Step 6: Check Results

At this stage, we check the results of the countermeasures implemented in the previous step. Checking the results means finding out how the control characteristics in question have changed since the countermeasures were implemented. The results should be measured in numerical terms, compared with the target values, and analyzed using QC tools to see whether or not the predicted improvements have been achieved. We must also compare the costs incurred with the benefits obtained and check whether or not any undesirable side-effects (adverse influences on other characteristics or previous or subsequent processes) have been produced.

The purpose of this step is to have everybody involved in the project identify and check the results they have achieved. Doing so gives them the satisfaction of reaching their targets, boosts their self-esteem, and enables them to experience a sense of personal growth and fulfillment and the pleasure of contributing to their company. It provides them with an opportunity to discover the thrill and excitement of successfully solving problems. This step consists of the following substeps:

Substep 1: Check results of improvements. Use the facts to check the effects of the improvements by gathering data on the results of the countermeasures with the aim of identifying the benefits obtained and analyzing these using QC tools. Also investigate any spin-off benefits. Stratify the data into data taken before and data taken after the improvements were effected, and compare the situation before and after using Pareto diagrams, histograms, and control charts. Also check whether the countermeasures have had any negative effects on quality, cost, delivery, efficiency, and so on, in other areas.

Substep 2: Compare results with target values. Compare the results of the countermeasures with the target values and identify the degree to which the target values have been achieved. If the degree of attainment of the targets is insufficient, return to Step 4 or Step 5.

Substep 3: Identify the benefits. Summarize the tangible benefits obtained from the improvements. It is a good idea to calculate the financial benefits as accurately as possible, since this provides a common yardstick for evaluating results.

The intangible benefits should be identified as well as the tangible ones. Some typical intangible benefits are as follows:

1. Understanding of problem-solving methodology has deepened, and problem-formulating and solving abilities have improved.

2. Leadership and teamwork have improved.
3. The QC mindset has taken hold.
4. Problem-consciousness, quality-consciousness, and improvement-consciousness have been raised.
5. Problem-solving activities have become self-starting.
6. People have become able to utilize the QC tools skillfully.
7. A cheerful, competent workplace has been created.

Case Study (*continued*)
9. *Check results.* As figure 4.9 shows, the effect of the various countermeasures implemented was to decrease the standard deviation of

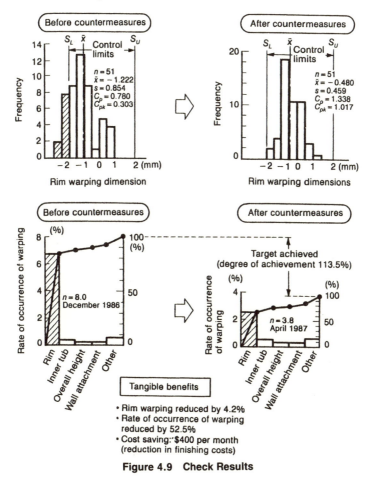

Figure 4.9 Check Results

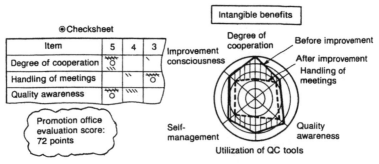

Figure 4.9—*Continued*

the rim-warping measurements, increase the process capability, and decrease the rate of occurrence of rim-warping defects (from 6.7 percent to 2.5 percent). The cost of finishing was also reduced by $400 per month, enabling us to achieve our targets.

Comment

The group members have checked the effects of their countermeasures and identified the results quantitatively. Comparing the situation before and after improvement using histograms and Pareto charts in this way makes the results immediately obvious.

The circle has also evaluated the intangible benefits of their problem-solving activities by plotting scores for degree of cooperation and degree of utilization of QC tools on a radar chart. This is a good way of quantifying intangible benefits.

Step 7: Standardize and Establish Control

The purpose of this step is to "apply the brakes" in order to lock our hard-won improvements into place and to prevent backsliding. It includes the twin aspects of standardizing and establishing control.

On receipt of our superior's approval, countermeasures accepted as effective are formally instituted as the new method of working. We must do this in order to maintain a state of control and ensure that we continue to obtain the desired results. To accomplish this, everyone must be made thoroughly conversant with the new work standards or production standards, education and training must be provided to enable them to become accustomed to the new working methods, and the control items (control characteristics) must be reviewed to enable us to check that the new methods are being correctly applied.

The following actions must be taken at this stage:

The QC Seven-Step Formula—Solving Problems the QC Way 105

Substep 1: Make the temporary standards official. In this substep, we ratify the temporary standards drawn up in Step 5 after any necessary revision. When doing this, we should observe the following points:

1. Clearly spell out all the key points.
2. Note in the revisions column the reason for and date of any revision.
3. Obtain the agreement of relevant work areas.
4. Obtain the approval of superiors.
5. Follow the official guidelines for establishing and revising company standards.

When setting a new standard, an in-house standard classification code should be obtained from the department responsible for controlling company standards.

Substep 2: Decide on the method of control. The benefits obtained from improvement activities must not be allowed to slip away. To make it possible to check whether or not the benefits of the improvements are being maintained and the improved situation is continuing, we must specify what control items and checkpoints should be used and how the process should be controlled. To do this, we must establish or revise control standards such as QC process charts, process abnormality countermeasure charts, and in-process defect control boards.

Substep 3: Disseminate the correct control methods thoroughly among everyone concerned. In this step, we hold special meetings or use the regular morning assemblies to explain the specified control methods and ensure that everybody affected is familiar with them.

Substep 4: Educate and train those responsible in the new working methods. We cannot expect the work to be done to standard if we do no more than hand over the new work standards to the workers and tell them to get on with it. Some workers will not read the standards carefully enough, while others will misunderstand them. Those in positions of authority must lead their subordinates by the hand and give them thorough education and training in the standards and the importance of obeying them.

Substep 5: Check whether the benefits are being maintained. In this substep we verify whether or not the new working methods are being followed and whether the improvement benefits are being maintained. QC tools such as checksheets, graphs, process capability charts, and control charts are used for this.

THE QC PROBLEM-SOLVING APPROACH

Process abnormalities can be classified into the following three types:

1. Abnormalities in control characteristics on control charts.
2. Product abnormalities, such as a sudden jump in numbers of defective articles.
3. Abnormalities to do with the 4 Ms, such as equipment failure.

If we discover a process abnormality, we must do something about the process or product as soon as possible. At the same time, we must track down the causes of the abnormality and take steps to prevent it recurring.

I would now like to discuss some important points for skillful standardization and establishment of control[10j].

Seven keys to skillful standardization and control

1. Raise everybody's quality-consciousness.   Good products and services never appear by chance. We have to make sure that each individual worker regards quality as important and feels responsible for it. We must raise everybody's awareness that quality is built in via the process.

Being quality-conscious means constantly striving to build in the required quality by following the laid-down quality standards and other standards.

2. Track down the causes of defects and mistakes and take action to prevent them recurring.   Whenever a process goes off the rails and generates defective products or mistakes, we must take appropriate action. In such cases, it is important not to be so concerned with the immediate problem that we restrict ourselves to stopgap measures. It is vital not just to take action to correct the defects in the product—that is, deal with the defective articles or mistakes—but also to hunt down the causes, find out why the defects or mistakes occurred in the first place, and take radical action to ensure that they never occur again through the same causes.

3. Lock the new working methods permanently into place.   To effect improvements, we have to do something about the 4 Ms (manpower, machines, materials, and methods), and this means that our working methods are naturally bound to change. We must therefore revise our work standards, QC process charts, action procedures, and other standards to ensure that the new working methods continue to be used.

4. Follow work standards closely.   Work standards are documents specifying the working methods needed to ensure that quality is built into the product via the process. Since they consist of standardized procedures

The QC Seven-Step Formula—Solving Problems the QC Way   107

designed to maintain the work at a uniform level, every worker must obey them faithfully. If these standards are not observed and each worker works as he or she happens to think fit, it will never be possible to provide goods or services of uniform quality.

5. Lock the control methods permanently into place.   Once we have effected an improvement, we must check the results to see if they were what we intended and find out whether or not any abnormalities are occurring as a result of some malfunction or other. If the results are not as we had hoped or abnormalities are present, we must take action. To ensure that this type of control action is carried out properly, we must specify how it should be done. Documents specifying control methods are called "control standards." In setting them, we must take care to answer the 5 Ws and 1 H in order to decide how data are to be collected and processed, how the normal and abnormal states are to be distinguished, what sort of corrective action is to be taken, and so on.

6. "Apply the brakes" by making use of control tools.   As in improvement activities, various tools are used to monitor the many assignable causes that make up a process and maintain the process in the controlled state or find out whether or not it is in that state. It is important to obtain good results by using effective standardization and control tools.

Customers are sometimes greatly inconvenienced as a result of trivial errors, and serious accidents may be caused by trifling slip-ups such as adding the wrong substance, writing down the wrong figure, or dropping something from a height. It is important to devise ways of eliminating such mistakes rather than simply tidying up the mess, shrugging our shoulders, and saying that such accidents are inevitable and nothing can be done about them. To help eliminate trivial mistakes, we must put a lot of effort into error-proofing. We should use the error-proofing approach to create the following mechanisms and methods:

• Mechanisms that allow equipment and processes to be handled without mistakes by amateurs.
• Working methods that anybody can execute correctly.
• Mechanisms that prevent mistakes when they appear likely to occur.

For an example of error-proofing, see p. 25.

7. Disseminate the new methods through education and training. However good the new standards or control methods may be, the workers will get

them wrong or fail to observe them if they are not thoroughly apprised of them. It is not good enough simply to hand over new standards and tell the workers to get on with the job. We must educate them in the reasons for the improvements and the key points of the new methods to ensure that they are thoroughly understood. When the workers have to master new skills in order to switch over to the new methods, they must also be given the necessary training.

Case Study (*continued*)

10. Standardize and establish control. At the same time that we were preparing workshop manuals, we drew up checksheets to be used for checking the torque wrenches and replacing the retaining bars. We decided to control the bathtub defect rate and rim-warping rate with QC control boards (graphs showing the state of control of each control characteristic daily and monthly) (see Table 4.10).

Table 4.10 Standardize and Establish Control

Why? (Objective)	What? (Item)	Who? (Leader)	Where? (Place)	How? (Method)	When? (Period)
Maintenance and control	Inspection of torque wrenches	Tamegai	Workplace	Check torque at start of work	Daily
	Periodic replacement of retaining bars	Kitanaka	Workplace	Standard replacement interval: once every 2 months (note on checksheet)	Every 2 months
Dissemination and familiarization	Work instructions, revisions to standards	Kojima	Training room, Workplace	Familiarize by means of work instructions and real-life models	10 May
Check progress of implementation	Quality level	Sugimoto	QC control board	Histogram	May–June
	Precision of curing jigs	Ono	Workplace	Checksheet (inspection)	31 May

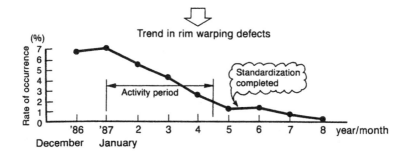

The QC Seven-Step Formula—Solving Problems the QC Way 109

11. Review and future directions.

- Bad points—some data were lacking and the analysis took a long time. Also, people did not say much during the meetings.
- Good points—we were able to use the QC tools and liaise well with other processes.
- Future activities—we intend to proceed with our activities in line with the annual plans, making use of the QC tools we mastered during this project. Our aim is to become better and better self-managers.

Comment

All the members of this circle participated fully in selecting a topic, carried out the project by proceeding through each of the steps in the QC Seven-Step Formula, and checked the benefits obtained. They are now sitting back and breathing a sigh of relief. If the circle now rests on its laurels without taking steps to lock the improvements into place, it will be like "carving a Buddha but leaving out the spirit"—in other words, the finishing touch will be missing. The circle must draw up regulations to ensure that the benefits continue to be maintained in the future. It must create a system to guarantee that the specific activities required for this are carried out.

Table 4.10 shows the "permanent fix" measures taken. The details of the standardization and control procedures were worked out by answering the 5 Ws and 1 H; designated people perform regular checks using checksheets and QC control boards, and submit reports. The systems devised for this are appropriately incorporated into the daily management of the work.

CHAPTER 5

The QC Tools

The QC approach to problem solving stresses the importance of collecting data that represent the true facts and analyzing these data in order to make accurate judgments. The QC tools are instruments for handling these data.

Dr. Kaoru Ishikawa, the leading figure in the development of QC in Japan, used to say that in his experience everybody could solve 95 percent of the problems around them by using the QC tools skillfully.

Making sure that everyone becomes thoroughly acquainted with simple QC tools and knows how to use them is more important than anything else in putting our finger on the nub of our problems.

5.1 The Significance of the QC Tools in the QC Problem-Solving Approach
You can't build a house without hammer and nails

Unearthing problems in the workplace, analyzing them, taking counter-measures, and establishing control requires some special tools unique to the QC problem-solving approach. One of QC's strongest features is the way in which it bases conclusions on hard data.

To put the maxim "Base everything on the facts" into effect, we should base our judgments and conclusions on numerical data. While we also need experience and intuition in order to perform our work, it is dangerous to rely on these alone. When we collect and analyze data, we often discover things we have not noticed when relying exclusively on intuition, and it becomes obvious that we were just guessing on the basis of our own limited experience without checking whether our guesses were accurate. Wishful thoughts such as "Decrease the defect rate" or "Increase satisfaction" repeated like incantations to the heavens will get us nowhere. However hard we

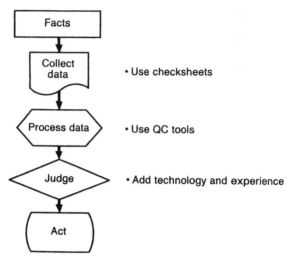

Figure 5.1 Using Data

work, we will never be able to produce the products we want if our machines are in poor condition or our raw materials are becoming contaminated.

To solve problems in the workplace, we must first find out exactly what is going wrong. This means painstakingly analyzing any nonconforming products or undesirable situations and examining the cause-and-effect system to pinpoint the true causes that are really affecting the results. This is where we need the QC tools (see Figure 5.1).

The QC tools are the third key to the QC problem-solving approach. They are our most important weapons in solving problems in the workplace.

In the QC problem-solving approach, it is important to start by gathering the kind of data that will help us grasp the facts. We then use such data to investigate the various factors (causes) considered to be affecting the results (characteristics), and check the relationships between the causes and the results. We analyze the data, effect countermeasures designed to produce more desirable outcomes, and control any factors that impair the results. The tools we use for analyzing and handling the data are known as the QC tools.

What Are the QC Tools?

The QC tools are techniques used in QC activities for discovering problems, organizing information, generating ideas, analyzing causes, taking action, effecting improvements, and establishing control.

The QC Tools   113

In this book, any technique that can be used effectively in quality control for dealing with data—both numerical and verbal—is defined as a QC tool.

Although the QC tools have been around for a long time, their effective use is still a much-discussed subject. It will continue to be important to use them widely in quality development, improvement, control, and assurance.

5.2 Individual QC Tools
The problem-solving toolbox

This section lists the various techniques used in QC problem solving and known collectively as the QC tools.

The QC Tools
(1)   The seven QC tools:

    (i) Cause-and-effect diagrams.
    (ii) Pareto diagrams.
    (iii) Graphs.
    (iv) Checksheets.
    (v) Histograms.
    (vi) Scatter diagrams.
    (vii) Control charts.

> Note: In *QC Sakuru Katsudo Un'ei no Kihon* (An Introduction to Managing QC Circle Activities) edited by the QC Circle Headquarters and published by the Union of Japanese Scientists and Engineers, graphs and control charts are treated as one item and stratification is added to the list. However, while it may be all right to include stratification in the list of tools, I think it is better to regard it as an approach rather than a tool. I also prefer to treat graphs and control charts separately, and this is why I have listed the seven QC tools as above.

(2)   Statistical methods:

    (i) Estimation and tests of hypotheses.
    (ii) Design of experiments (analysis of variance, orthogonal arrays, etc.).
    (iii) Correlation analysis (simple correlation analysis, multiple correlation analysis).
    (iv) Regression analysis (simple regression analysis, multiple regression analysis).

114   THE QC PROBLEM-SOLVING APPROACH

    (v) Orthogonal polynomials.
    (vi) Binomial probability paper.
    (vii) Simple analytical methods.
    (viii) Multivariate analysis techniques (Principal-component analysis, factor analysis, clustering and discrimination, quantification Types I–IV, etc.).
    (ix) Optimization methods (simplex method, Box–Wilson method, EVOP, etc.).

(3) The seven new QC tools:

    (i) Relations diagrams.
    (ii) Systematic diagrams.
    (iii) Matrix diagrams.
    (iv) Affinity diagrams.
    (v) Arrow diagrams.
    (vi) Process decision program charts.
    (vii) Matrix data analysis.

(4) Other QC methods:

    (i) Sampling techniques.
    (ii) Sampling inspection.
    (iii) Sensory inspection.
    (iv) Reliability engineering (FTA, FMEA, Weibull probability paper, cumulative hazard paper, etc.).

(5) Methods peripheral to QC:

    (i) IE techniques.
    (ii) VE techniques.
    (iii) OR techniques.
    (iv) Idea-generating strategies.

    The QC tools used in solving problems range from simple methods such as drawing graphs to sophisticated techniques requiring computers for their application.
    Tools used in QC circle or QC team activities should satisfy the following conditions:

    1. They should be easy to use. Do not make people use tools that re-

quire difficult calculations or complicated drawings; use ones that can be mastered in a few hours of study.
2. They should be easy to understand. Use tools that are immediately comprehensible visually.
3. They should be capable of being used by everyone together. For QC circle or group activities, select tools that are used by everybody working together.

The seven QC tools satisfy the above conditions, and Table 5.1 gives an overview of them. They are not described in detail in this book, but readers requiring further information on preparing, interpreting, and using them are referred to another of the author's books, *QC Nanatsu Dogu—Yasashii QC Shuho Enshu* (The Seven QC Tools—A Seminar in Easy QC Methods), published in 1982 by the Union of Japanese Scientists and Engineers.

It is important for everyone to become thoroughly familiar with the use of the simpler QC tools—the so-called Seven QC Tools—to analyze routine data taken from the workplace, stratified data, and data obtained from experiments, based on the concept of dispersion and the statistical approach. The Seven New QC Tools, statistical estimation and tests of hypotheses, analysis of variance, and other techniques should also be used depending on the objectives and the nature of the problem.

Table 5.2 shows the principal uses of the QC tools and the areas where they are likely to give the best results in solving the various problems that we find around us.

Table 5.1 An Overview of the Seven QC Tools

Seven QC Tools	Description	Method of use	Remarks
Pareto diagrams	A diagram on which undesirable events or costs associated with items such as quality (e.g. number of defects or non-conforming products), productivity, cost, safety and so on are stratified according to their causes or manifestations and plotted in order of importance.	There may be a large number of undesirable phenomena or causes of trouble. The Pareto diagram makes it easy to see which of these have the most serious effect on quality, productivity, cost, safety, etc., together with their relative proportions.	Plot the "other" category at the far right of the diagram and ensure that it is not too large.
Cause-and-effect diagram	A diagram shaped like the bones of a fish for systematically summarizing the relationships between quality characteristics, defects, etc. and their causes.	Useful for searching out the factors that affect the characteristics, sorting out the relationships between these factors (causes) and the characteristics (the results), and depicting these systematically.	Gather the opinions of as many people as possible in order to flush out all the relevant factors.
Graphs and charts	Diagrams for plotting data and showing temporal changes, statistical breakdowns and relationships between different quantities.	Used for organizing data. Use line graphs for showing time trends, bar graphs for comparing quantities and pie charts for showing relative proportions.	Use solid lines, dotted lines, circles and crosses skillfully for clarity.
Checksheets	Forms specially prepared to enable data to be collected simply by making check marks.	Used for tallying the occurrences of the defects or causes being addressed and graphing or charting them directly.	Clarify the objective and design a checksheet to suit it.
Histograms	Prepared by dividing the data range into subgroups and counting the number of points in each subgroup. The number of points (the frequency) is then plotted as a height on the diagram.	Prepare separate, stratified histograms for each of the 4Ms and examine the relationships between the shapes of the distributions and the specifications.	Use at least 30 values, preferably around 100.
Scatter diagrams	Prepared by plotting paired sets of data such as hardness and tensile strength, temperature and yield, porosity and insulation resistance, etc. against each other on x and y axes.	Collect paired sets of data on causes and effects, and use scatter diagrams to check for correlation between the sets of data.	Use at least 30 values, 50 if possible.
Control charts	Prepared by plotting time along the horizontal axis and a characteristic value on the vertical axis. Unlike line graphs, they also show the control limit lines.	Use to check whether there are too many chronic defects, too much variation, values lying outside the control limits, or undesirable trends or cycles. Control charts show whether or not a process is in control.	Think about the best method of stratification and pay close attention to subgrouping.

The QC Tools

Table 5.2 QC Tools and Their Uses

Type of Tool	Tool	Main use	New-product and new-technology development	Quality, cost and delivery improvement	Process control	Market surveys, information management	Administration	Sales management	Service management	Environmental protection and safety management
The Seven QC Tools	Cause-and-effect diagrams	Picking up and arranging all possible causes without any omissions	○	◉	○	○	◉	◉	◉	◉
	Pareto diagrams	Singling out the really serious problems from among all the lesser ones.	○	◉	○	○	◉	◉	◉	◉
	Graphs and charts	Making data visual	○	○	○	○	◉	◉	◉	◉
	Checksheets	Simplifying data collection and ensuring that no items are omitted when inspecting	○	○	◉	○	◉	◉	◉	◉
	Control charts	Checking whether or not a process is in control	○	○	◉	○				○
	Histograms	Plotting the shape of a distribution and comparing it with specifications	○	◉	◉		◉	◉	◉	◉
	Scatter diagrams	Finding correlation between paired sets of data	○	◉	○		○	○	○	○
Statistical Tools	Estimation and tests of hypotheses	Estimating populations and deciding whether to accept or reject hypotheses	○	◉	○					○
	Design-of-experiment techniques	Planning experiments rationally and analyzing data economically and precisely	◉	◉		○				○
	Correlation analysis	Investigating correlation between variables		○						
	Regression analysis	Investigating functional relations between variables	◉	◉		○				○
	Orthogonal polynomials	Breaking down and analyzing variation in factors	○	○		○	○			○
	Binomial probability paper	Estimating and testing hypotheses		○		○				○
	Simple analytical techniques	Estimating and testing hypotheses by simple calculation using large amounts of data		○						○
	Multivariate analysis	Summarizing relationships among large numbers of variables and clarifying their structure.	◉	◉	◉	◉	○	○	○	
	Optimization	Identifying strategies that will enable systems or processes to be operated in their optimal state		○	○					○

Table 5.2—Continued

Type of Tool	Tool	Main use	New-product and new-technology development	Quality, cost and delivery improvement	Process control	Market surveys, information management	Administration	Sales management	Service management	Environmental protection and safety management
The Seven New QC Tools	Relations diagrams	Elucidating complex problems by identifying logical connections	O	O			O	O	O	O
	Systematic diagrams	Systematically searching for the most effective means of accomplishing given objectives	◉	◉		O	O	O	O	O
	Matrix diagrams	Clarifying problems through multidimensional thinking	◉	◉		O	O	O	O	O
	Affinity diagrams	Unearthing problems by organizing data on chaotic situations	O	O						
	Arrow diagrams	Controlling schedules by expressing relationships among tasks in the form of a network	O	O						
	Process decision program charts	Determining the process to be used to achieve the desired results	O	O	O					O
	Matrix data analysis	Arranging data in matrix form for easy visualization and comprehension	O	O		O				
Other QC Tools	Sampling techniques	Determining the nature and state of a population by taking samples	O	O	O	O	O	O	O	O
	Sampling inspection	Judging whether to accept or reject a lot in accordance with a particular sampling plan		O	O					O
	Sensory inspection	Inspecting using the physical senses	O	O	O	O			O	
	Reliability engineering	Maintaining a machine's functions rationally throughout its expected life cycle	◉	O	O		O			O
	IE techniques	Achieving the required quantity and quality at the most appropriate cost in the stipulated time		O			O	O	O	O
	VE techniques	Reducing costs by analyzing the value of products from the functional aspect	O	O						
	OR techniques	Providing decision-makers with quantitative solutions to problems	O			O				O
Peripheral to QC Techniques	Creativity engineering	Developing people's creativity	◉	O		O	O	O	O	O

Note: ◉: particularly effective O: effective

5.3 How to Use the QC Tools
A system for becoming a skillful user of the QC tools

To create delicious dishes in the kitchen, it is important to follow the correct procedure. When making a beef stew, for example, we should take the following steps:

1. Prepare the vegetables and cut the beef into chunks.
2. Heat some butter in a frying pan, fry the beef rapidly, and remove it from the pan.
3. Add some more butter to the frying pan and fry the onions, then add the rest of the vegetables. . .

The reasons why we fry the meat before stewing it is that this seals its surface and prevents the juices from escaping. The stew will not be so tasty if we get the procedure wrong.

Following the correct procedure is also important when using the QC tools. The basic procedure for using the QC tools is described below.

Basic Procedure for Skillful Use of QC Tools
Step 1: Establish objective
1. Understanding the situation.
2. Analysis.
3. Checking results.
4. Control.
5. Inspection.
6. Adjustment.

We will waste our efforts if we start collecting data without knowing why we are collecting it.

Step 2: Select tool
Once we have decided on our objective, we must consider which tools are applicable and select the most appropriate one.

Step 3: Collect data
Before starting to collect data, we should ask ourselves the 5 Ws and 1 H:

1. How many readings do we need?
2. Over what period should we collect the data?
3. How should we stratify the data?

THE QC PROBLEM-SOLVING APPROACH

4. What sampling or measurement methods should we use?
5. Who should collect the data, when should they collect it, and what process should they collect it from?

> Note: The data referred to in this step are generally quantitative—either by variable or by attribute. However, when cause-and-effect diagrams or relations diagrams are used, the data collected is usually verbal.

Step 4: Analyze data using QC tool

In this step, we analyze the data using the tool selected in Step 2. If this analysis fails to yield any useful information, we either return to Step 2 or analyze the data using a different tool and compare the results.

Step 5: Consider results and derive conclusions

We then consider the analytical results of the previous step in conjunction with other technical information and experience, and draw conclusions.

Step 6: Act

In this step, we take some specific action.

1. When we have understood the situation→set improvement targets.
2. When we have identified the cause of a problem→think up counter-measures.
3. When we have been able to confirm results→standardize if the results are good.
4. When we have been able to identify the state of control→take action if there are any abnormalities, and maintain the status quo if there are none.
5. When we have found defective articles by inspection→remove defective articles or reject unacceptable lots.
6. When we have found that a process requires adjustment→adjust it so as to bring it back within the control limits.

5.4 The QC Seven-Step Formula and the QC Tools
Use the right tool at the right time

Table 5.3 and Figure 5.2 show which of the seven QC tools should be used at each step in the QC Seven-Step Formula when addressing problems in the workplace.

As mentioned earlier, "QC tools" refers not only to the Seven QC Tools

The QC Tools

Table 5.3 Use of the Seven QC Tools in the QC 7-Step Formula

No.	Step		Pareto diagrams	Cause-and-effect diagram	Graphs and charts	Check-sheets	Histograms	Scatter diagrams	Control charts
1	Select Topic		◎	O	O	O	O		O
2	Understand Situation and Set Targets	Understand situation	O	◎	◎	O	O		O
		Set targets	O		◎		O		O
3	Plan Activities				◎				
4	Analyze Causes	Investigate relationship between causes and characteristics		◎				O	
		Investigate past and present situations	O		◎	O	◎		◎
		Stratify	O	O	O	O	◎	◎	◎
		Investigate temporal changes			O				◎
		Investigate mutual relationships	O		O			◎	
5	Consider and Implement Countermeasures			◎	O				
6	Check Results		O		O	O	◎		◎
7	Standardize and Establish Control				O	◎	O		◎

Note: ◎: particularly effective; O: effective

but also to the Seven New QC Tools, statistical estimation and tests of hypotheses, correlation analysis, sampling techniques, design-of-experiment techniques, and so on. I would like to see everybody studying all of these tools as well as VE, IE, and other methods.

Since the Seven QC Tools are relatively simple, it is easy to learn how to prepare the required charts or diagrams with a little study. Their application, however, is not so easy. One of the most difficult things appears to be deciding what kind of data to collect in order to understand a phenomenon and its causes accurately.

Merely being able to stand up in front of a class and talk about how to apply the QC tools does not mean that one has mastered them to any great extent. All things considered, the best way to learn about problem solving is to get to grips with real workplace problems and sweat them out.

122 THE QC PROBLEM-SOLVING APPROACH

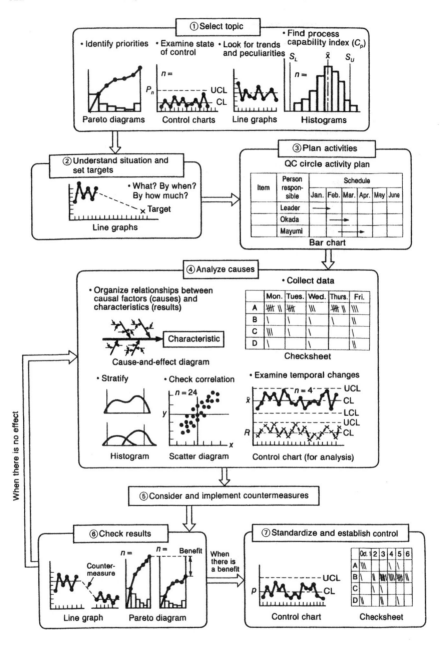

Figure 5.2 The QC 7-Step Formula and the Seven QC Tools

The QC Tools

This is why Dr. Kaoru Ishikawa, the inventor of QC circles, used to advise people to study the QC tools not intellectually but by hands-on experience, using their physical senses. The best way to improve our skills is to take the QC tools we have studied and actually apply them in the workplace. This is the only way to really understand them, and it will also show up our weaknesses and stimulate us to take the initiative and study hard to make up for any deficiencies.

Finally, I would like to summarize the seven key points in applying the QC tools:

1. Make full use of the simpler QC techniques, that is, the Seven QC Tools.
2. Clarify the nature of the data, that is, the method of stratification, sampling, measurement, and so on.
3. Use various tools in combination.
4. Carefully examine analytical results from the technical standpoint.
5. Study the QC tools well and understand them correctly.
6. Have faith in the QC tools; realize that good improvement and control are impossible without them.
7. Take the tools you have learned and try them for yourself; get a feeling for them in practice.

5.5 Using the QC Tools as Part of the QC Seven-Step Formula
Make good use of the seven QC tools

It is important to select and use the appropriate QC tool at each stage as the problem-solving activities gradually unfold, selecting the tools that best suit our objective. In other words, we must learn how to use the QC tools in conjunction with the QC Seven-Step Formula. Some case studies are described below to illustrate the use of the tools as part of the QC Seven-Step Formula.

Step 1: Select Topic
1. Outline the process
When describing the background to the topic, we should first outline the process. A convenient way of doing this is to diagram the process using the "Graphical Symbols for Process Charts" (JIS Z 8206) shown in Tables 5.4 and 5.5. Table 5.4 shows the basic symbols used for depicting the process elements themselves, while Table 5.5 shows the auxiliary symbols used for showing the relationships between process elements.

124 THE QC PROBLEM-SOLVING APPROACH

Table 5.4   Basic Graphic Symbols for Process Charts

No.	Process element	Title of symbol	Symbol	Meaning	Remarks
1	Process-ing	Process-ing	○	Indicates a process that changes the shape or properties of raw materials, working materials, parts or products.	
2	Trans-portation	Trans-portation	○	Indicates a process that alters the position of raw materials, working materials, parts or products.	The diameter of the "transportation" symbol is to be 1/2–1/3 of that of the "processing" symbol. The symbol ⇨ may be used in place of the symbol ○; however, the latter symbol does not indicate the direction of transportation.
3	Stag-nation	Storage	▽	Indicates a process in which raw materials, working materials, parts or products are stored according to plan.	
4		Conges-tion	D	Indicates an unplanned state of congestion of raw materials, working materials, parts or products.	
5	Inspec-tion	Quantity inspection	□	Indicates a process in which the quantity or number of raw materials, working materials, parts or products is measured, and the result is compared with a standard in order to find the difference.	
6		Quantity inspection	◇	Indicates a process in which a quality characteristic of a raw material, working material, part or product is tested, and the result is compared with a standard in order to decide whether a lot is acceptable or rejectable or an individual product is conforming or non-conforming.	

Figure 5.3 shows a process in a glass factory. The improvement topic selected was "Reduce Costs by Reviewing the Amount of Silica Sand Used"[6]. Its aim was to reduce raw materials costs. This example shows how a complex process can be made easy to understand by the skillful use of diagrams.

Table 5.5 Auxiliary Graphical Symbols for Process Charts

No.	Name of symbol	Symbol	Meaning	Remarks
1	Flow line	│	Indicates sequential relationships among process elements.	When a sequential relationship is unclear, its direction shall be clearly indicated by drawing an arrow at the end or in the mid-region of the flow line. Intersections of flow lines shall be indicated by
2	Division	∿∿	Indicates control boundaries in a series of processes.	
3	Omission	═══	Indicates the omission of part of a series of processes.	

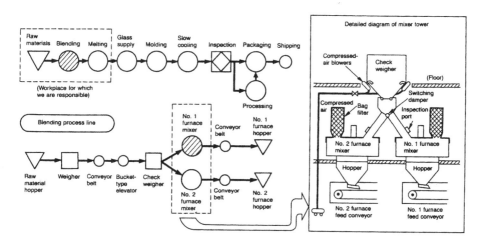

Figure 5.3 Description of a Process Using Process Symbols

2. Decide on the topic

Topics are usually closely related to the work we do and are found by examining particular operations that are causing trouble. Matrix diagrams are often used to examine the many problems identified and to narrow them down to a single improvement topic.

Mitsuyo Shinohara and his colleagues are responsible for issuing invoices for repairs to electronic measuring instruments. They put their heads together to discuss the problems they were experiencing in their work, thought up seven items for evaluating them, and prepared the matrix diagram shown

Item weighting	Item score × 1			Item score × 2					
Problem \ Item	Commonality of topic	Ease of tackling	Ease of data collection	Degree of urgency	Degree of importance	Relevance to department policy	Predicted benefits	Total score	(Points) 0 10 20 30 40 50 60
Support can only be provided for communal jobs	O	Δ	×	O	Δ	×	O	37	
Many justified complaints	Δ	×	O	Δ	O	×	Δ	33	
Order forms slow in arriving	O	Δ	O	O	O	O	O	53	
Work of previous process not understood	O	×	×	Δ	Δ	×	O	23	
Too much credit given	Δ	×	Δ	O	O	O	Δ	43	

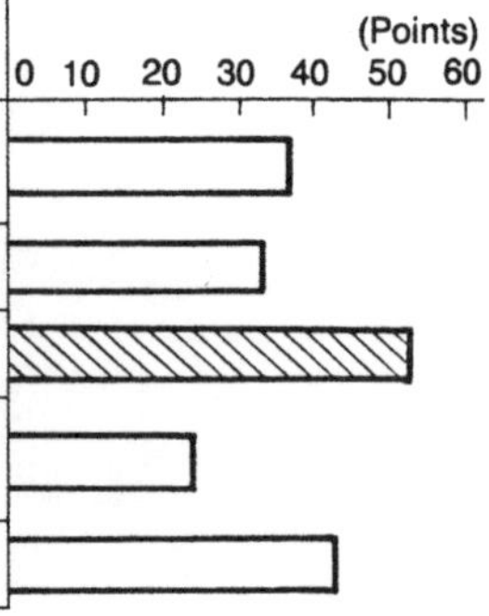

Topic Selection Evaluation Chart

Scoring scheme: O ... 5 points   Δ ... 3 points   × ... 1 point

Figure 5.4   Topic Selection Using Matrix Diagram

in Figure 5.4[10e]. This showed that the most serious problem was that it was taking too long for the order forms to arrive, and they decided to tackle the topic of "Reducing the nonarrival rate of order forms in the repair of electronic measuring instruments."

Step 2: Understand Situation and Set Targets

Line graphs are helpful for tracking the past behavior of the object of the improvement activities—that is, the control characteristic.

A tunnel construction site office plotted the number of leaks per 100 m^2 after completing the first phase of the construction work (see Figure 5.5). The graph showed a large number of leaks in the side walls. This was thought to be because the excavation was irregular and deep and the ground was soft. It not only failed to satisfy the quality requirements of the customer but also was running up large repair costs.

It was therefore decided to set the improvement targets shown below. The aim was to reduce the number of leaks by improving the construction method.

- Control characteristic . . . average number of leaks per 100 m^2.
- Target . . . 21.4→10.0.
- Period . . . by July 1989.

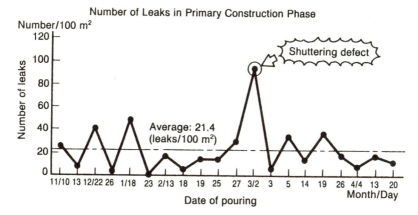

Figure 5.5 Understanding Situation Using Line Graph

Step 3: Plan Activities

To plan our improvement activities, we must prepare a detailed, precise action plan. The bar chart is one of the easiest and most convenient tools for this purpose.

Figure 5.6 shows an action plan prepared by the reception staff for outpatients in the department of internal medicine at a certain hospital. The staff had noticed that the average waiting time per patient between arrival at reception and being seen by the doctor was as long as 95 minutes, and they decided to address this problem by selecting as their topic "Reduce Outpatients' Waiting Times in the Department of Internal Medicine."

Problem-Solving Activity Plan

Topic: Reduce Outpatient Waiting Times in
Department of Internal Medicine   Circle name: White-Hat Circle

Step	What? Action item	Who? Leader	By when? (period) April	May	June	July	Aug.	How? Action taken
1	Select topic	All members (6)	▭ ▪					We selected a topic that was very pertinent to outpatient reception in the department of internal medicine and reflected the hospital manager's policy of improving service to patients.
2	Understand situation and set targets	Michiura, Tada	▭ ▪					We measured, over a 20-day period, the time taken by patients from arriving at reception to being seen by a doctor.

Note: ▭ Planned, ▪ Implemented

Figure 5.6 Bar Chart Activity Plan

Step	What? Action item	Who? Leader	By when? (period) April	May	June	July	Aug.	How? Action taken
3	Plan Activities	Sono		□ ■				We shared out the workload among all the circle members and appointed a leader for each step.
4	Analyze Causes	Kishihara, Michiura		□	■			We identified the principal causes from a cause-and-effect diagram and analyzed patients' actions and times taken.
5	Consider and Implement Counter-measures	Watanabe				□ ■		We implemented countermeasures such as reducing the writing of slips to a single operation, preparing charts explaining test procedures to patients, and speeding up the writing of prescriptions by providing stick-on drug labels.
6	Check Results	Tada				□ ■		We checked the results by drawing histograms for waiting times and line graphs for patients' complaints.
7	Standardize and Establish Control	Ikeda				□ ■		We prepared work manuals, test procedure sheets, checklists for preventing prescription omissions, and so on.

Note: □ Planned, ■ Implemented

Figure 5.6—*Continued*

Step 4: Analyze Causes

1. Summarize relationships between characteristics and causes

The cause-and-effect diagram is the most effective tool for this. Figure 5.7 shows a cause-and-effect diagram prepared by all the members of a quality circle at an Osaka hospital specializing in kidney diseases[10f]. This diagram lists the possible causes for the large number of mistakes in transcribing prescriptions. As their topic, the circle selected "Reduce the Number of Mistakes in Transcribing Prescriptions."

2. Check differences between strata

Stratify the data according to the 4 Ms, prepare graphs, histograms, scatter diagrams, and control charts, and check for differences between different strata.

In one case, a group examined data on a certain welding process in order to see whether there was a relationship between the welding sequence and the bending that was being produced by the welding[10g]. They prepared separate histograms for welding the flange first and welding the web first. These histograms, shown in Figure 5.8, showed that when the flange was welded first, there was a marked difference in the contraction of the upper

The QC Tools

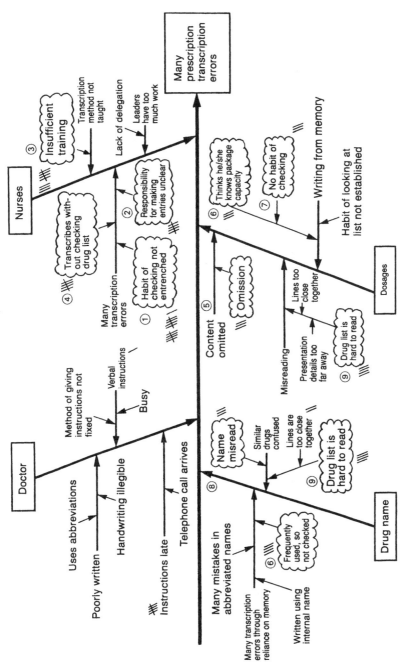

Figure 5.7 Organizing Causes on a Cause-and-Effect Diagram

130 THE QC PROBLEM-SOLVING APPROACH

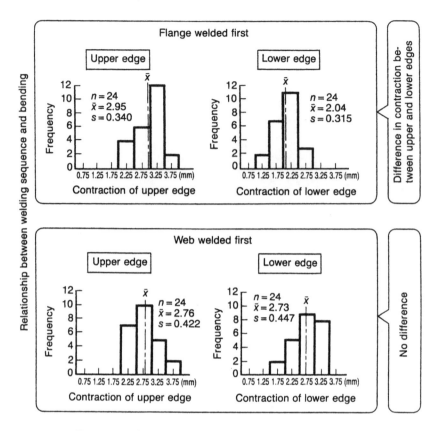

Figure 5.8 Comparing Stratified Data Using Histograms

and lower edges. This difference was causing the excessive bending. It had been commonly accepted, based on the advice of experienced steel specialists, that it was best to weld the flange first, but the result of this analysis clearly showed that it was in fact better to weld the web first.

3. Investigate temporal changes

Graphs or control charts are used to examine changes with time. One group performed an experiment in which they incorporated an insulating plate into a die in order to raise its temperature during the casting of camera bodies. As Figure 5.9 shows, they discovered from this that the temperature of the die rose faster when the insulating plate was used and that a steady-state temperature 20°C higher could be obtained.

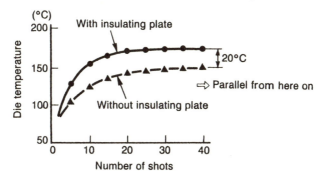

Figure 5.9 Investigating Time Changes Using Graphs

4. Check for correlation

Scatter diagrams can be used to check whether or not any correlation exists between two sets of data.

One group prepared a scatter diagram to see whether there was a relationship between the depth of the hole in an injector ring and the amount of material ejected[10h]. As Figure 5.10 shows, the amount ejected was dipping below the lower specification, even though the depth of the holes satisfied the existing standards on the drawings. As a result of this investigation, the group decided to narrow the gap between the specifications for the hole depth and to take action to reduce the dispersion in the depth.

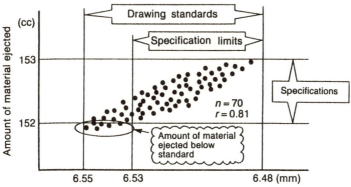

Figure 5.10 Investigation of Correlation Using Scatter Diagram

132   THE QC PROBLEM-SOLVING APPROACH

Step 5: Consider and Implement Countermeasures

The tools used in this step include systematic diagrams, matrix diagrams, affinity diagrams, process decision program charts, cause-and-effect diagrams for pursuing countermeasures, and idea-generating strategies.

Figure 5.11 shows an example of the use of a systematic diagram to evaluate proposals for improving the environment of a design office. Figure 5.12 shows an example in which the drawings section in the technical administration department of a research laboratory used idea-generating strategies to come up with proposals for issuing drawings and design documents in a more timely fashion[10i]. Stimulating our creativity in this way by using idea-generating strategies to question ourselves enables us to come up with some excellent plans.

Step 6: Check Results

Histograms, control charts, graphs, and Pareto charts are effective for checking the results of improvements.

In a process for assembling industrial robots, the process capability for an important quality characteristic, the speed-reducer axle deflection, was insufficient. In an attempt to improve this, the group analyzed the factors affecting the machining precision of parts and took countermeasures, such as reducing the dispersion in the internal diameter and angular outside diameter of the speed-reducer casing (factors greatly affecting the deflection), modifying the method of fastening the lower manipulator arm, and so on.

Figure 5.13 was prepared to illustrate the effect of these countermeasures. After the improvements, the control chart showed a state of control and the histogram showed a process capability index (Cp) of 1.64, indicating that a satisfactory process capability had been obtained.

Step 7: Standardize and Establish Control

In this step, the countermeasures seen to be effective are standardized, and tools such as graphs and control charts are used to check whether a state of control is being maintained.

In constructing the pumping station for a certain industrial park, it was found possible to improve the efficiency of the pile-driving work by measures such as "Improve the Deckplates" and "Modify the Attachment for False Piles." The QC process chart and work procedures were revised on the basis of this and the process was analyzed using an $x-Rs$ process chart. This chart, illustrated in Figure 5.14, was then used to control the process from pile no. 61 on[7].

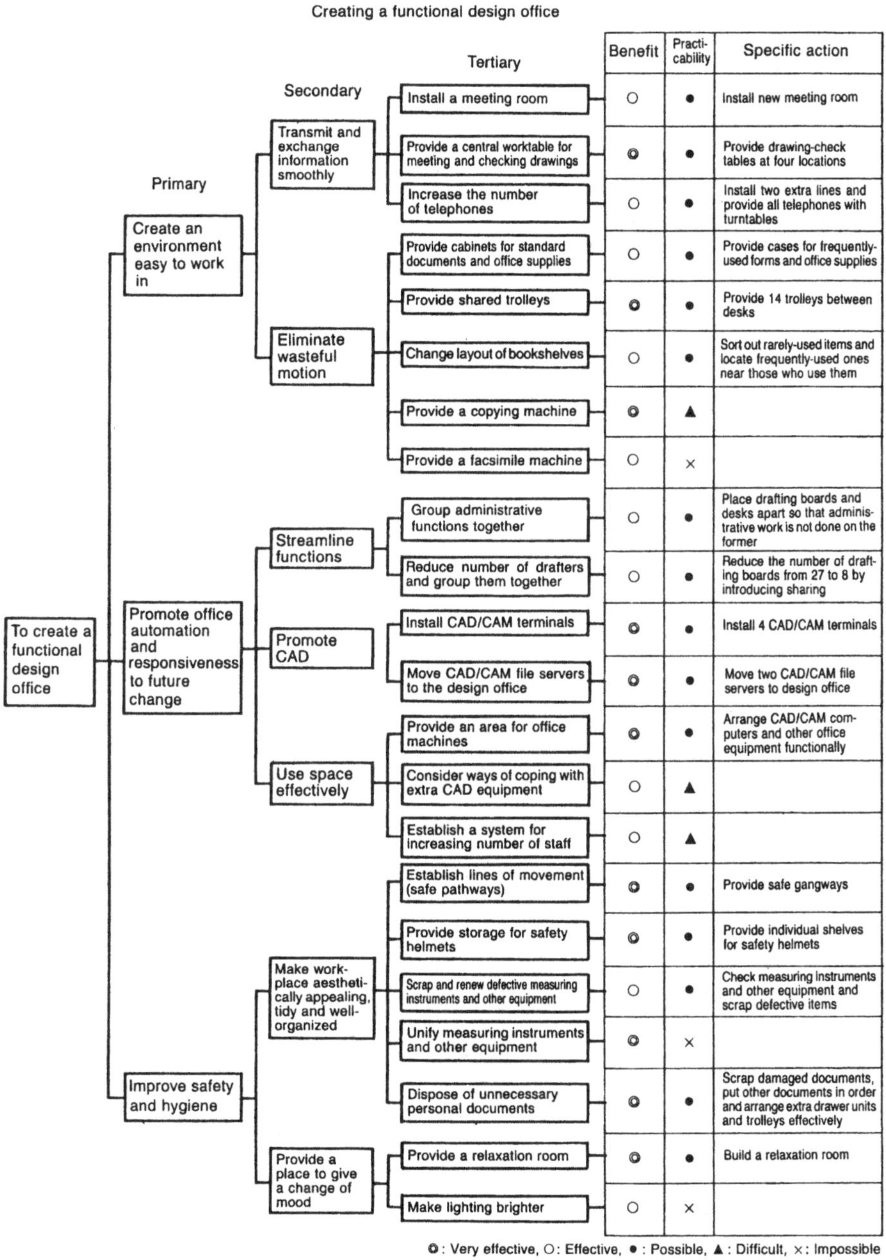

The QC Tools

Creating a functional design office

To create a functional design office	Primary	Secondary	Tertiary	Benefit	Practi-cability	Specific action
		Secondary	Install a meeting room	O	●	Install new meeting room
	Create an environment easy to work in	Transmit and exchange information smoothly	Provide a central worktable for meeting and checking drawings	◎	●	Provide drawing-check tables at four locations
			Increase the number of telephones	O	●	Install two extra lines and provide all telephones with turntables
			Provide cabinets for standard documents and office supplies	O	●	Provide cases for frequently-used forms and office supplies
		Eliminate wasteful motion	Provide shared trolleys	◎	●	Provide 14 trolleys between desks
			Change layout of bookshelves	O	●	Sort out rarely-used items and locate frequently-used ones near those who use them
			Provide a copying machine	◎	▲	
			Provide a facsimile machine	O	×	
To create a functional design office	Promote office automation and responsiveness to future change	Streamline functions	Group administrative functions together	O	●	Place drafting boards and desks apart so that administrative work is not done on the former
			Reduce number of drafters and group them together	O	●	Reduce the number of drafting boards from 27 to 8 by introducing sharing
		Promote CAD	Install CAD/CAM terminals	◎	●	Install 4 CAD/CAM terminals
			Move CAD/CAM file servers to the design office	◎	●	Move two CAD/CAM file servers to design office
			Provide an area for office machines	◎	●	Arrange CAD/CAM computers and other office equipment functionally
		Use space effectively	Consider ways of coping with extra CAD equipment	O	▲	
			Establish a system for increasing number of staff	O	▲	
	Improve safety and hygiene	Make work-place aesthetically appealing, tidy and well-organized	Establish lines of movement (safe pathways)	◎	●	Provide safe gangways
			Provide storage for safety helmets	◎	●	Provide individual shelves for safety helmets
			Scrap and renew defective measuring instruments and other equipment	O	●	Check measuring instruments and other equipment and scrap defective items
			Unify measuring instruments and other equipment	◎	×	
			Dispose of unnecessary personal documents	◎	●	Scrap damaged documents, put other documents in order and arrange extra drawer units and trolleys effectively
		Provide a place to give a change of mood	Provide a relaxation room	◎	●	Build a relaxation room
			Make lighting brighter	O	×	

◎ : Very effective, O : Effective, ● : Possible, ▲ : Difficult, × : Impossible

Figure 5.11 Evaluating Countermeasures Using a Systematic Diagram

134 THE QC PROBLEM-SOLVING APPROACH

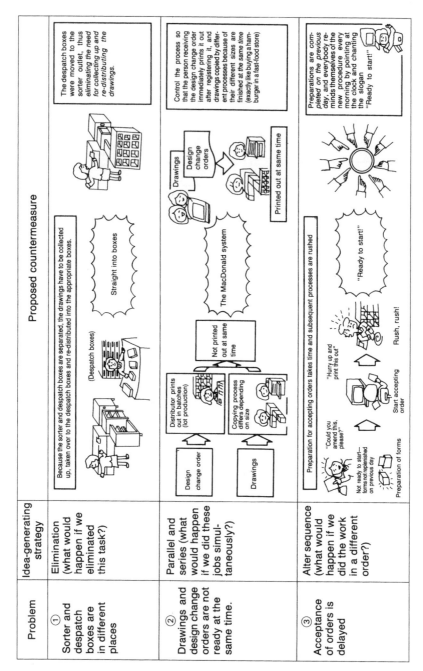

Figure 5.12 Devising Countermeasures Using Idea-Generating Strategies

The QC Tools   135

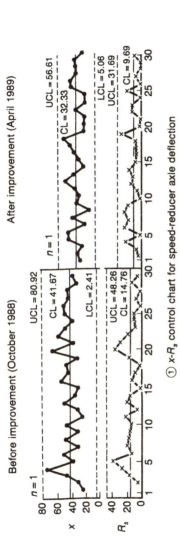

① x-R_s control chart for speed-reducer axle deflection

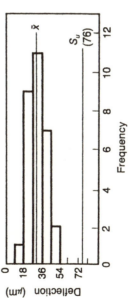

② Histogram for speed-reducer axle deflection

Minimum: 13.0
Maximum: 48.0
Average: 30.83
Standard deviation: 9.21
C_p: 1.64

After improvement, the process was stable and the process capability satisfactory

Figure 5.13   Checking Results with Control Charts and Histograms

136 THE QC PROBLEM-SOLVING APPROACH

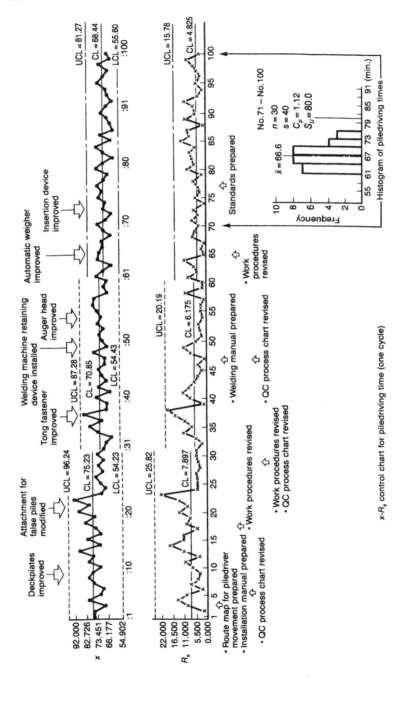

Figure 5.14 Establishing Control by Means of x-R_s Control Charts

CHAPTER 6

Some Examples of the QC Problem-Solving Approach

Without teaching and learning, people do not grow. Children learn from their parents, pupils from their teachers, and less experienced workers from more experienced workers.

Exactly the same thing applies to the QC problem-solving approach. It is hoped that readers will use the case studies presented in this chapter to study how to tackle problems and how to use the QC tools.

It is important continually to repeat the cycle of study and practical application. True problem-solving ability is only acquired by getting to grips with problems ourselves and building up our own hands-on experience.

6.1 The QC Story
The secret of preparing improvement activity reports

Whenever a QC circle, QC team, or other workplace group carries out improvement activities, they should always prepare a written report of these activities. The benefits of this can be seen from the following list of seven reasons for preparing reports:

1. It makes people review their activities and plan for the future.
2. It provides useful information for other groups and individuals and encourages them to try similar activities.
3. Reports constitute a concise record of the activities carried out and thus help the organization to accumulate experience and technology.
4. It improves people's writing skills and makes workers more confident and more knowledgeable.
5. Summarizing and reviewing the activities boosts the group's team spirit and gives its members a sense of achievement.

138   THE QC PROBLEM-SOLVING APPROACH

6. It improves people's ability to use the right **QC** tool for the right purpose.
7. It helps raise the standards of QC circle and **QC** team activities.

When preparing QC reports, it is a good idea to follow the *QC Story* format.

The QC Story is the format to be followed when a QC circle or team reports on the results of improvement or problem-solving activities.

A story must have a plot. Reporting improvement or problem-solving activities in story form enables the results to be communicated intelligibly and pithily.

The standard format for the QC Story, often used for reporting on QC circle activities or presenting the results obtained by a QC team, is shown in Table 6.1.

Table 6.1   The QC Story and the QC 7-Step Problem-Solving Formula

The Basic Steps in the QC Story

Step 1   Introduction
Step 2   QC Circle Introduction
Step 3   Outline of Process

Step 4   Reasons for Selecting Topic
Step 5   Understand the Situation
Step 6   Set Targets
Step 7   Plan Activities
Step 8   Analyze Causes
Step 9   Consider and Implement Countermeasures
Step 10   Check Results
Step 11   Standardize and Establish Control

Step 12   Reflections and Future Directions

the steps in the box correspond to those of the QC 7-Step Problem-Solving Formula

When writing a QC Story, the following seven points should be observed:

1. Decide on a framework and clarify the main points you want to get

Some Examples of the QC Problem-Solving Approach 139

across, the key points of the activities, and anything else you want to emphasize. Stories that have no climax and do not appeal to the reader are not very gripping.

2. Make use of diagrams and pictures to get your message across visually—a picture is worth a thousand words. It is important to free people from having to make the effort to read by presenting figures and phenomena in graphic form.

3. Keep sentences short and use lists whenever possible—long sentences, like stodgy food, are hard to digest.

4. Avoid long words and technical jargon—use simple language.

5. Use headings, subheadings, and punctuation effectively—it is important to make your material easy to read, just as arranging food artistically makes it more appetizing.

6. Put yourself in your readers' shoes and write plainly—avoid long-winded explanations and do your best to write directly about facts and processes from the reader's standpoint.

7. Write accurately and intelligibly—do not embellish the facts. Dramatizing always makes for implausibility.

6.2 Announcing the Results of Problem-Solving Activities
Use presentation meetings to keep tabs on improvement and personal growth

It is important to announce the results of group activities such as QC circle or QC team activities to others at presentation meetings or symposia. The purpose of publicizing the results of one's activities like this is to invite comments from superiors and other departments, and to provide a forum for self-evaluation, leading to self-improvement and mutual enlightenment.

I would now like to give seven hints for skillful presentation—an important part of QC circle activities—together with some tips for writing good reports.

1. Make sure the presentation gives information on concrete activities such as the analysis of causes using QC tools, original and creative improvement ideas, thoughts on how to run the circle better, and so on.

2. Using the QC Story as a framework, emphasize the special features of the activities, talk about the difficulties encountered, and mention the parts played by the circle members.

3. Avoid technical jargon, talk convincingly, and make the presentation easy for the audience to understand.
4. Use overhead projector slides or wallcharts effectively.
5. Practice the presentation several times and be sure to speak clearly and pleasantly.
6. Strictly observe the time limit.
7. When answering a question, make sure you know what is being asked, and reply succinctly.

Some Tips for Preparing Problem-Solving Activity Reports
- Keep the report coherent, following the format: Problem→Cause→Countermeasure→Results.
- Restrict the length of the report to two to four standard $8\frac{1}{2} \times 11$ pages.
- Number and title all figures and tables.
- Record the date when each of the main steps was started.

1. Topic
- Whenever possible, describe topics in the following terms:

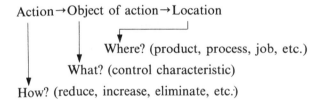

Example 1: Reduce the in-process defect rate in the electronics parts shop.

- If necessary, provide a subtopic (e.g., an interesting finding or point of appeal) below the main topic in smaller characters. *Example 2:* Subtopic for example 1: Analyzing data using the Seven QC Tools.

2. Reasons for selecting topic
- Clearly and concisely state the objective and necessity of taking up this particular problem. Do not give a lengthy explanation of the background. The reasons for selecting the topic and the background leading up to the decision to tackle the topic are easily confused, but starting the discussion a long way from the actual topic (i.e., describing the background) makes the story overcomplicated—the opposite of what is required.

Some Examples of the QC Problem-Solving Approach   141

• The topic must be a serious problem. Explain the connection between the topic and the policy to which it relates, mentioning what that policy is.
• It is usually sufficient merely to list the reasons for selecting the topic when the length of the report is restricted to a few pages; if space permits, however, it is best to include graphs or diagrams illustrating the objective and necessity of the topic. (Note: not including these in the report does not mean that the data are not needed.)

3. **Understand situation**
   • Use graphs to illustrate past trends in the subject of the problem-solving activities (the control characteristics) selected for setting the targets.
   • Examine the undesirable phenomenon under consideration from the following four angles and give a simple, illustrated explanation of the problem.
   Time—when the problem occurs (time of day, date, day of the week, week, month, etc.).
   Place—where the problem occurs (division, process, operating unit, geographical area, etc.; position of defective product or part, location of defect on product or part).
   Model—product model or type of part.
   Phenomenon—appearance of defect, etc. (e.g., in paint defects; runs, pools, bare patches, etc.).
   • Some people find it difficult to grasp the difference between understanding the situation and analyzing the causes. The best way to think of understanding the situation is "investigating the undesirable phenomenon only, from various angles," and analyzing the causes as "investigating the relationship between the undesirable phenomenon and any deficiencies in the working methods" (i.e., checking out the 4 Ms and the cause-and-effect system). The cause-and-effect system (Who? By what method? With what material? With what tools? On what machines? and so on) should not be considered in the "Understand the Situation" step but in the next step, "Analyze Causes."

4. **Set targets**
   • "Setting targets" means selecting the control characteristics to be used as criteria for assessing whether or not the situation taken up as the topic (the problem) has improved, specifying the levels to be reached, and stipulating the date by which they are to be reached.
   • Targets should be expressed in terms of results (something expressing quality, cost, and delivery of products or work). Avoid expressing them

142   THE QC PROBLEM-SOLVING APPROACH

in terms of the process (number of times performed, number of items, etc.). *Example:*

Topic: Improve technicians' skills.

Good target: Skill rating.

Poor target: Number of classes held, number of trainees attending, etc.

- A well-set target should answer the three questions: "What?," "By when?," and "By how much?"

5. Analyze causes

- If possible, list at least thirty possible causes on both a cause-and-effect diagram and a relations diagram. The most important point here is for the diagrams to show clearly that the true causes have been identified.
- Use the item identified as the problem in the "Understand situation" step as the characteristic on the cause-and-effect diagram. If this is not done, the point of the "Understand situation" step will be lost and the QC Story will break down.
- On graphs and charts (cause-and-effect diagrams, etc.) showing analytical results, always note the date when the analysis was performed.
- The "Analyze causes" step is for investigating the relationships between characteristics and causes. Describe how corresponding sets of data on characteristics and causes were collected from the workplace and tested, and what experiments were performed. Even when tests show no correlation, provide graphs and tables comparing data on characteristics and causes, or charts contrasting the results of opinion surveys, questionnaires, and other investigations with areas requiring improvement, clearly showing how the true causes were singled out. Only beginners with an elementary grasp of QC leap straight from drawing the cause-and-effect diagram to implementing countermeasures.

6. Consider and implement countermeasures

- In this step, describe the countermeasures taken, making clear what was actually done. Action lies at the heart of continuous improvement (*kaizen*). It is the only thing that actually raises a company's standard.
- It is no good trying to put on a show by providing only a hastily drawn systematic diagram for countermeasure proposals and leaving it at that. Specific details of the actions taken (illustrated by charts and diagrams, partial diagrams of forms, photographs, illustrations, etc.) must be given.
- It is surprising how often countermeasures are aimed at causes other than the important ones identified on the cause-and-effect diagram. When this is done, the point of analyzing the causes is lost and the QC

Some Examples of the QC Problem-Solving Approach 143

Story falls apart. Make sure there is a clear correspondence between causes and countermeasures.

7. Check results

- In this step, be sure to check the results with the same control characteristics as used for setting the targets, so that the results can be compared with the target values. It is not unusual to find different characteristics being used to check the results from those used to set the targets. Do not introduce extra indicators not used for setting the original targets.
- Separate the results into "Tangible Benefits" and "Intangible Benefits."

8. Standardize and establish control

- Establishing control means checking and ensuring that the countermeasures are being repeated and sustained so that the benefits achieved by the improvement activities are not lost. Standardization, on the other hand, means institutionalizing the new methods that produce those benefits and making them a permanent company asset.
- If new systems have been introduced or old ones modified, this must be noted: that is, we must mention whether new working methods developed as a result of the countermeasures undertaken have been standardized in the form of work procedures and manuals; whether work flow diagrams have been revised; whether existing control items have been modified or new ones added; and whether the relevant people have been informed and trained.
- When recording the fact that a standard has been established, revised, or abolished, be sure to include its title and number.

9. Reflections and future directions

- In this step, we write down our thoughts on how the activities were performed and the next round of issues that should be addressed within the scope of the particular topic.

6.3 Some Problem-Solving Case Studies
Learning from good examples

In solving problems, we must use our own initiative and take the lead in helping ourselves and others to develop our talents. But how, specifically, should we go about it? This chapter tries to answer this question by introduc-

144   THE QC PROBLEM-SOLVING APPROACH

ing the following three case studies, each an excellent example of the QC problem-solving approach:

Case Study 1: Improving Precision of Load Capacity Measurement for Drive Springs.

Case Study 2: Reducing Number of Hang-Ups in Switchboard Operation.

Case Study 3: Ensuring Sufficient Adhesion in Direct Application of Tiles to Concrete.

When studying these examples, please take special note of the following six points:

1. How the topic was selected.
2. How the PDCA Wheel was rotated in proceeding to solve the problem.
3. How the causes were analyzed.
4. How countermeasures were planned and implemented.
5. The particular difficulties experienced and how they were overcome.
6. How the case studies are organized and presented.

I hope that readers will obtain some useful hints from these examples, take them back to their QC circles or groups, and utilize them in solving problems.

Some Examples of the QC Problem-Solving Approach 145

Case Study 1: Improving Precision of Load Capacity Measurement for Drive Springs

Hirokazu Kitamura, Controller Group, Quality Control Division, Daihen Co., Ltd.

1. Introduction

Our company, Daihen, manufactures and sells electrical equipment such as transformers, various kinds of welding machines, welding robots and so on. Our quality circle, the Schalter Circle, belongs to the Controller Group in the Quality Control Division. We are responsible for incoming inspection of parts for the tap switchgear built into large transformers.

2. Reasons for Selecting Topic

① There was a large variation in the measurements of the drive spring loading capacity, making it difficult to decide whether to accept or reject them.
② If an out-of-spec spring is passed on to the next process, this impairs the performance of the selector switch.
③ Improving measurement precision is one of our section's policies.

3. Activity Plan

-- → Plan,　── → Action

Step⟍　　　　　Month	May 1988	June	July	August
Understand Situation	--→			
Analyze Causes		---‑--→		
Consider and Implement Countermeasures			--‑-→	
Check Results				---‑--→
Standardize and Establish Control				--‑→

Outline of Schalter Circle

Outline of Circle		Composition of Circle		
QC circle registration number	*13700*	*6*		
Date of formation	*April 1982*	Number of members	6 men	
Number of subscriptions to QC magazines taken out by circle members	*1*		0 women	
			0 part-timers	
Name of circle leader	*Hirokazu Kitamura*	Ages of members	Average age: *43.5*	
Length of time as leader	*2 years 2 month*		Oldest: *52*	
			Youngest: *28*	

Details of Circle Meetings		Status of Circle Activities	
Number of meetings held per month	Number of regular meetings lasting 30 minutes or longer: *4*	Number of topics completed since formation of circle	Major topics: *16*
	Number of short meetings lasting 20 minutes or less: *0*	Number of topics completed in past year	Major topics: *4* Minor topics: *0*
Average time taken per regular meeting	*90* minutes	Average time spent per topic	*4* months
Average attendance rate at regular meetings	*100*%	Main items addressed	/safety/ cost/morale/
Principal meeting place	Meeting room/workplace/outside company		

Presentation methods: leaflets / OHP / other (　　)

146 THE QC PROBLEM-SOLVING APPROACH

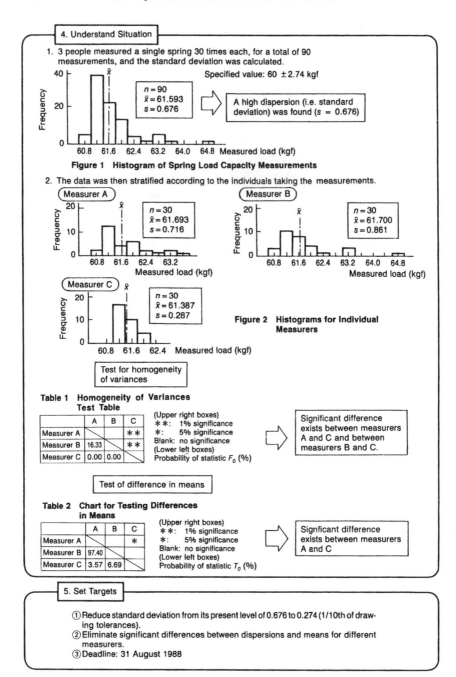

Some Examples of the QC Problem-Solving Approach

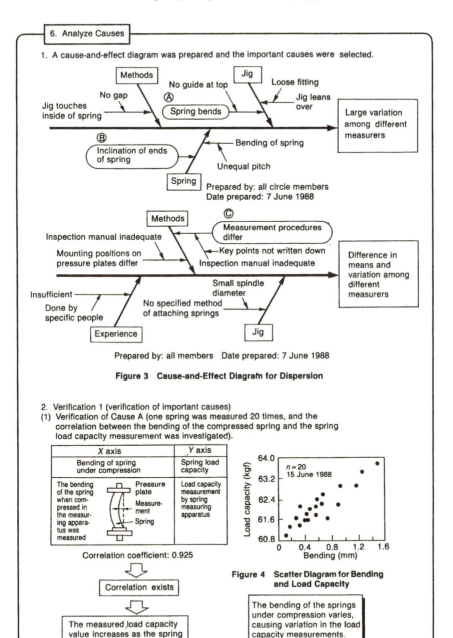

6. Analyze Causes

1. A cause-and-effect diagram was prepared and the important causes were selected.

Figure 3 Cause-and-Effect Diagram for Dispersion

2. Verification 1 (verification of important causes)
(1) Verification of Cause A (one spring was measured 20 times, and the correlation between the bending of the compressed spring and the spring load capacity measurement was investigated).

Figure 4 Scatter Diagram for Bending and Load Capacity

148   THE QC PROBLEM-SOLVING APPROACH

(2) Verification of Cause B (the inclination of the end-faces of 20 springs was measured and the correlation between this and the standard deviation of the measured spring load capacities was investigated)

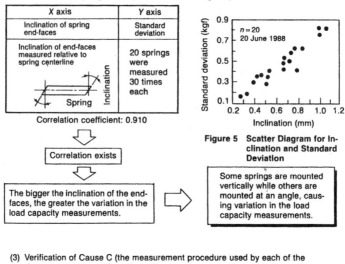

X axis	Y axis
Inclination of spring end-faces	Standard deviation
Inclination of end-faces measured relative to spring centerline	20 springs were measured 30 times each

Correlation coefficient: 0.910

⇩

Correlation exists

⇩

The bigger the inclination of the end-faces, the greater the variation in the load capacity measurements.

Figure 5 Scatter Diagram for Inclination and Standard Deviation

⇨ Some springs are mounted vertically while others are mounted at an angle, causing variation in the load capacity measurements.

(3) Verification of Cause C (the measurement procedure used by each of the three measurers was investigated)

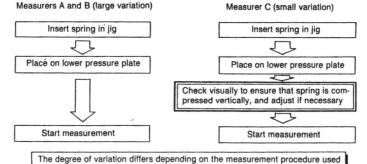

Measurers A and B (large variation)

Insert spring in jig
⇩
Place on lower pressure plate
⇩
Start measurement

Measurer C (small variation)

Insert spring in jig
⇩
Place on lower pressure plate
⇩
Check visually to ensure that spring is compressed vertically, and adjust if necessary
⇩
Start measurement

The degree of variation differs depending on the measurement procedure used

3. Verification 2 (difference in load capacity due to difference in mounting of spring)

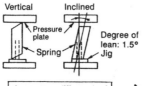

Vertical   Inclined
Pressure plate
Spring   Degree of lean: 1.5°
            Jig

Units: kgf

	Vertical	Inclined	Difference
1st	61.1	64.5	3.4
2nd	61.2	64.3	3.1
3rd	61.3	64.7	3.4
Average	61.2	64.5	3.3

An average difference of 3.3 kgf was discovered

⇨ The load capacity differs depending on whether the spring is mounted vertically or at an angle

7. Consider and Implement Countermeasures

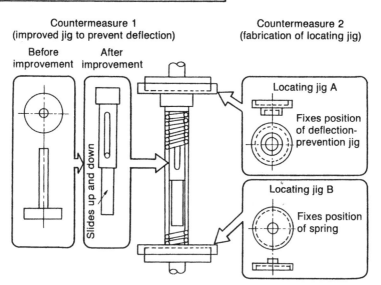

Countermeasure 1
(improved jig to prevent deflection)

Countermeasure 2
(fabrication of locating jig)

Results of countermeasures

(1) The improved deflection-prevention jig eliminated the bending of the springs under compression
• Bending of spring compressed 20 times (mm)

	Maximum	Minimum	$\bar{x}$
Before countermeasures	1.35	0.10	0.51
After countermeasures	0.30	0.05	0.12

(2) The springs could now be compressed parallel to the compression direction

Measurements for 20 springs		Maximum	Minimum	$\bar{x}$
	Angle of lean	0.3°	0.1°	0.2°
	Spring load capacity	61.6 (kgf)	60.9 (kgf)	61.1 (kgf)

(3) Fixing the positions of the jig and the spring eliminated differences in how different measurers mounted the springs on the measuring apparatus

150 THE QC PROBLEM-SOLVING APPROACH

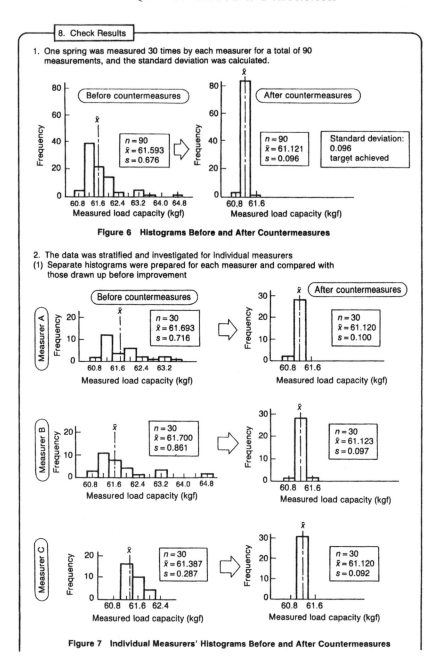

Figure 6 Histograms Before and After Countermeasures

Figure 7 Individual Measurers' Histograms Before and After Countermeasures

Some Examples of the QC Problem-Solving Approach

(2) Differences between individual measurers were investigated

Before countermeasure

Table 3 Test of Homogeneity of Variance

	A	B	C
Measurer A			∗∗
Measurer B	16.33		∗∗
Measurer C	0.00	0.00	

(Upper right boxes)
∗∗: 1% significance
∗: 5% significance
Blank: no significance

Table 4 Test of Difference in Means

	A	B	C
Measurer A			∗
Measurer B	97.40		
Measurer C	3.57	6.69	

(Upper right boxes)
∗∗: 1% significance
∗: 5% significance
Blank: no significance

After countermeasures

	A	B	C
Measurer A			
Measurer B	89.16		
Measurer C	68.99	79.27	

(Lower left boxes)
Probability of statistic F_0 (%)

	A	B	C
Measurer A			
Measurer B	89.64		
Measurer C	100.00	89.25	

(Lower left-boxes)
Probability of statistic t_0 (%)

The differences between individual measurers were eliminated and the target was achieved

---

9. Standardize and Establish Control

1. Inspection Manual S209 was revised by adding instructions for use of jigs during measurement of drive spring load capacities.
2. A new jig control standard (QPS-012-SU) was prepared and is to be used for jig inspection and maintenance.

---

10. Evaluate and Reflect

1. Evaluation .... In our role as inspectors, we take a serious view of variation in measurements. Taking this as our topic for the present improvement project and solving the problem together gave us enormous pleasure and greatly improved our teamwork.
2. Reflection .... Because our activity plan for analyzing the causes was inadequate, we had a large number of items to verify and missed our deadline. In future, we intend to proceed by obtaining clear answers to the 5W's and 1H at each step.

Case Study 2:

Improvement Activity Report	Topic: Reducing Number of Hang-Ups in Switchboard Operation
Procedure — P (Plan): 1. Reasons for Selecting Topic 2. Understand Situation (to provide a basis for setting targets) 3. Set Targets (What? By how much? By when?)	D (Do): 1. Analyze Causes (survey past and present data, analyze and elucidate causes) 2. Consider and Implement Countermeasures

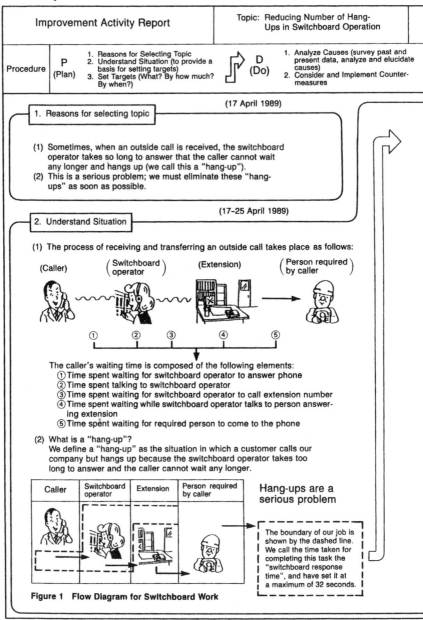

Figure 1 Flow Diagram for Switchboard Work

Some Examples of the QC Problem-Solving Approach   153

Period of Activities: 17 April 1989–30 June 1989	Circle: "Hello, Hello" Circle, General Affairs Division, Osaka Office, Maeda Construction Co., Ltd.	In charge: Tsukawaki Katao

C
(Check)
1. Check Results (investigate results of countermeasures and degree of attainment of targets)
2. Identify Benefits (tangible and intangible)

A
(Act)
1. Standardize (set new standards or revise old ones, specify method of sustaining improvements)
2. Establish Control (ensure that improved situation is being maintained)
3. Identify Remaining Problems

(3) We divided the hour between 9:00 and 10:00 a.m. into 5-minute periods and counted the number of outside calls received during each period, as shown in Fig. 2. We also counted the number of hang-ups during the day of the survey (21 April), and these are shown in Table 1.

Sometimes 4 or 5 outside calls arrive simultaneously

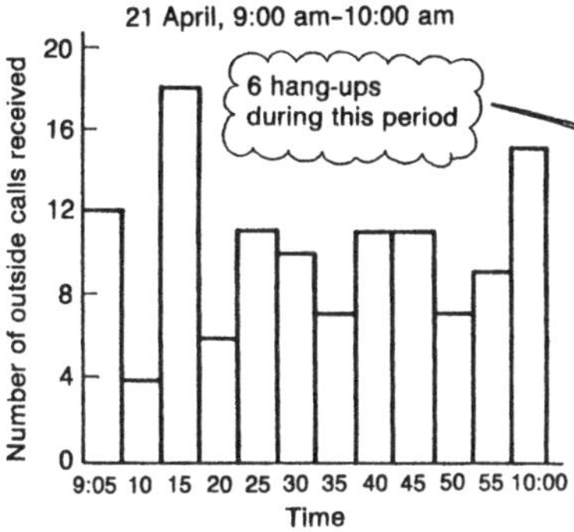

21 April, 9:00 am–10:00 am

6 hang-ups during this period

Figure 2   Bar Chart for Numbers of Outside Calls

Table 1   Number of Hang-Ups (21 April)

Time period	Number of calls	Number of hang-ups
8:30 ~ 9:00	27	3
9:00 ~ 10:00	121	6
10:00 ~ 11:00	111	1
11:00 ~ 17:00		
17:00 ~ 17:30	33	1
Total	535	13

(4) Figure 3 shows the number of hang-ups occurring each day between 17 and 21 April

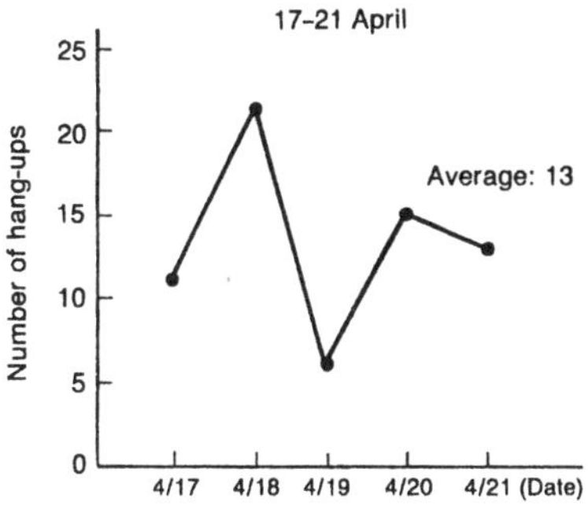

17–21 April

Average: 13

Figure 3   Line Graph for Outside-Call Hang-Ups

26 April 1989

3. Set Targets

Reduce number of outside-call hang-ups from average of 13 per day to 6 per day by end of June

Down to 6!

Go! Go! Go! Get those hang-ups down!

154   THE QC PROBLEM-SOLVING APPROACH

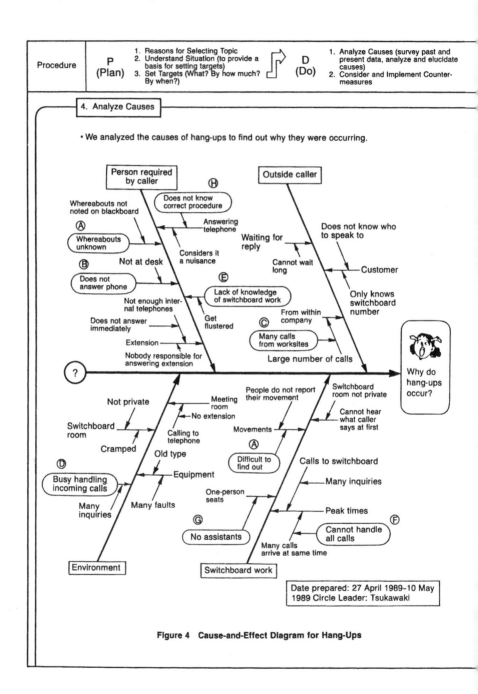

Figure 4 Cause-and-Effect Diagram for Hang-Ups

Some Examples of the QC Problem-Solving Approach   155

 1. Check Results (investigate results of countermeasures and degree of attainment of targets)
(Check) 2. Identify Benefits (tangible and intangible)

 1. Standardize (set new standards or revise old ones, specify method of sustaining improvements)
(Act) 2. Establish Control (ensure that improved situation is being maintained)
3. Identify Remaining Problems

27 April–31 May 1989

Ⓐ We further investigated a particular cause of hang-ups; lack of knowledge about people's movements within the company

We counted the number of outside calls coming into the switchboard at various times of day and plotted them on the graph shown in Fig. 5

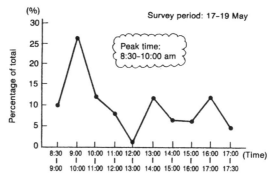

Figure 5   Relative Frequencies of Outside Calls at Different Times of Day

We counted the number of people posted as "out" on their workplace's In/Out board and compared this with the number of people actually out.

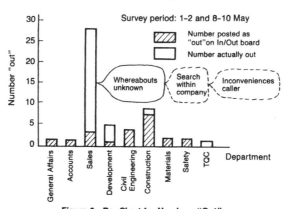

Figure 6   Bar Chart for Numbers "Out"

Findings
(1) Peak time for outside calls arriving at switchboard starts at 8:30 a.m.
(2) Number of people posted as "out" on In/Out boards differs from number actually out
(3) Difference in numbers shown on Fig. 6 means extra switchboard time
(4) This difference in numbers leads to hang-ups and inconveniences outside callers

156   THE QC PROBLEM-SOLVING APPROACH

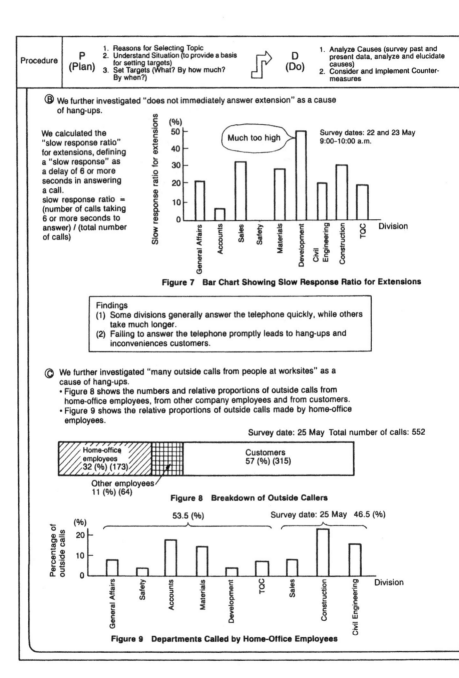

| Procedure | P (Plan) | 1. Reasons for Selecting Topic
2. Understand Situation (to provide a basis for setting targets)
3. Set Targets (What? By how much? By when?) | ⇒ | D (Do) | 1. Analyze Causes (survey past and present data, analyze and elucidate causes)
2. Consider and implement Counter-measures |

(B) We further investigated "does not immediately answer extension" as a cause of hang-ups.

We calculated the "slow response ratio" for extensions, defining a "slow response" as a delay of 6 or more seconds in answering a call.
slow response ratio = (number of calls taking 6 or more seconds to answer) / (total number of calls)

Survey dates: 22 and 23 May 9:00–10:00 a.m.

Figure 7 Bar Chart Showing Slow Response Ratio for Extensions

Findings
(1) Some divisions generally answer the telephone quickly, while others take much longer.
(2) Failing to answer the telephone promptly leads to hang-ups and inconveniences customers.

(C) We further investigated "many outside calls from people at worksites" as a cause of hang-ups.
• Figure 8 shows the numbers and relative proportions of outside calls from home-office employees, from other company employees and from customers.
• Figure 9 shows the relative proportions of outside calls made by home-office employees.

Survey date: 25 May Total number of calls: 552

Home-office employees 32 (%) (173) | Customers 57 (%) (315)
Other employees 11 (%) (64)

Figure 8 Breakdown of Outside Callers

Figure 9 Departments Called by Home-Office Employees

C (Check)
1. Check Results (Investigate results of countermeasures and degree of attainment of targets)
2. Identify Benefits (tangible and intangible)

 A (Act)
1. Standardize (set new standards or revise old ones, specify method of sustaining improvements)
2. Establish Control (ensure that improved situation is being maintained)
3. Identify Remaining Problems

Findings
(1) A large proportion of outside calls are from company employees and 32% of them are from home-office employees alone.
(2) 46.5% of home-office employees calling in could use direct lines to do so.
(3) The 173 outside calls made by home-office employees shown in Figures 8 and 9 could thus be reduced by 80 per day (173 × 0.465).

Ⓓ We further investigated "too many calls directed to operators" as a cause of hang-ups.
• We investigated two types of call to operators: "inquiries" and "asking for messages".

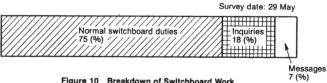

Survey date: 29 May

Normal switchboard duties 75 (%) — Inquiries 18 (%)

Messages 7 (%)

Figure 10 Breakdown of Switchboard Work

Findings
(1) 25% of all outside calls are directed to switchboard operators
(2) 25% of these could be switched through to the relevant division, reducing the number of inquiries dealt with by operators

Ⓔ Lack of understanding of switchboard operators' duties—prepare explanatory notes for employees.
Ⓕ Many calls arrive at once—reduce number of calls on outside lines
Ⓖ Nobody helps with switchboard work—arrange for two new female company entrants from the General Affairs Division to help at busy times
Ⓗ People answering extensions ignorant of correct procedure—switchboard operators will prepare and distribute simple instructions for answering telephone

158   THE QC PROBLEM-SOLVING APPROACH

| Procedure | P (Plan) | 1. Analyze Causes (survey past and present data, analyze and elucidate causes) 2. Consider and Implement Countermeasures | D (Do) | 1. Reasons for Selecting Topic 2. Understand Situation (to provide a basis for setting targets) 3. Set Targets (What? By how much? By when?) |

5. Consider and Implement Countermeasures

(1–30 June 1989)

Cause No.	Analysis	Countermeasure
Ⓐ	Time is wasted searching for people who are out of the office because it is not known who is actually in or out at any given time.	Circulate a request to every division asking people to make proper use of their In/Out boards. (a)
Ⓑ	Extension phones are often left to ring six or more times before finally being answered.	Prepare and circulate "Extension-Phone Answering Duties". (b)
Ⓒ	Outside calls from people at worksites can be reduced to around 80.	Circulate written requests to all worksites. (c)
Ⓓ	Switch outside calls directed to operators through to relevant departments, reducing operator time per call.	Prepare and distribute "Extension-Phone Answering Duties"
Ⓔ	Make persistent efforts to have people understand.	Prepare and distribute "Extension-Phone Answering Duties"
Ⓕ	Install more direct lines to reduce the number of calls coming through the switchboard.	Submit request form to General Affairs Division Manager. (d)
Ⓖ	Arrange for two extra staff (new female company entrants from General Affairs Division)	Give assistants 2 weeks' training.
Ⓗ	Strive to have everyone answer the telephone expertly.	Prepare and distribute "Extension-Phone Answering Duties"

To All Divisions

(a)

Mr. Inoue

Request for Proper Notification of Whereabouts

Established: 30 June 1989
Effective from: 30 June 1989

Standard for Answering
Extension Phones   (b)

Authority: General Affairs Division, Osaka Office

To All Worksites

(c)

Request to Use Direct Lines

2 June 1989

To: Mr. Kashiwada

Request for Installation of
New Direct Lines

(d)   16 June 1989

Switchboard Operators Tsukawaki, Katao

Some Examples of the QC Problem-Solving Approach   159

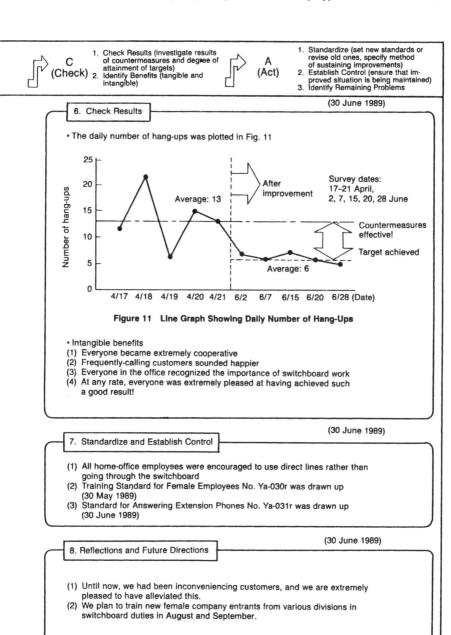

C (Check)
1. Check Results (investigate results of countermeasures and degree of attainment of targets)
2. Identify Benefits (tangible and intangible)

A (Act)
1. Standardize (set new standards or revise old ones, specify method of sustaining improvements)
2. Establish Control (ensure that improved situation is being maintained)
3. Identify Remaining Problems

(30 June 1989)

6. Check Results

- The daily number of hang-ups was plotted in Fig. 11

Survey dates:
17–21 April,
2, 7, 15, 20, 28 June

Countermeasures effective!
Target achieved

Figure 11   Line Graph Showing Daily Number of Hang-Ups

- Intangible benefits
(1) Everyone became extremely cooperative
(2) Frequently-calling customers sounded happier
(3) Everyone in the office recognized the importance of switchboard work
(4) At any rate, everyone was extremely pleased at having achieved such a good result!

(30 June 1989)

7. Standardize and Establish Control

(1) All home-office employees were encouraged to use direct lines rather than going through the switchboard
(2) Training Standard for Female Employees No. Ya-030r was drawn up (30 May 1989)
(3) Standard for Answering Extension Phones No. Ya-031r was drawn up (30 June 1989)

(30 June 1989)

8. Reflections and Future Directions

(1) Until now, we had been inconveniencing customers, and we are extremely pleased to have alleviated this.
(2) We plan to train new female company entrants from various divisions in switchboard duties in August and September.

THE QC PROBLEM-SOLVING APPROACH

Case Study 3:

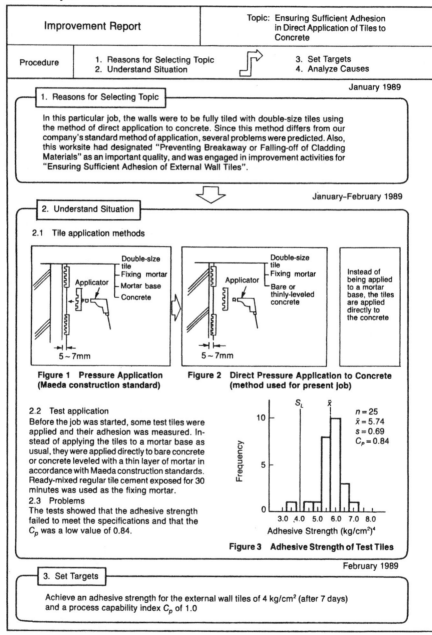

Improvement Report	Topic: Ensuring Sufficient Adhesion in Direct Application of Tiles to Concrete
Procedure	1. Reasons for Selecting Topic 2. Understand Situation 3. Set Targets 4. Analyze Causes

1. Reasons for Selecting Topic

January 1989

In this particular job, the walls were to be fully tiled with double-size tiles using the method of direct application to concrete. Since this method differs from our company's standard method of application, several problems were predicted. Also, this worksite had designated "Preventing Breakaway or Falling-off of Cladding Materials" as an important quality, and was engaged in improvement activities for "Ensuring Sufficient Adhesion of External Wall Tiles".

2. Understand Situation

January–February 1989

2.1 Tile application methods

Figure 1 Pressure Application (Maeda construction standard)

Figure 2 Direct Pressure Application to Concrete (method used for present job)

Instead of being applied to a mortar base, the tiles are applied directly to the concrete

2.2 Test application
Before the job was started, some test tiles were applied and their adhesion was measured. Instead of applying the tiles to a mortar base as usual, they were applied directly to bare concrete or concrete leveled with a thin layer of mortar in accordance with Maeda construction standards. Ready-mixed regular tile cement exposed for 30 minutes was used as the fixing mortar.

2.3 Problems
The tests showed that the adhesive strength failed to meet the specifications and that the C_p was a low value of 0.84.

$n = 25$
$\bar{x} = 5.74$
$s = 0.69$
$C_p = 0.84$

Figure 3 Adhesive Strength of Test Tiles

3. Set Targets

February 1989

Achieve an adhesive strength for the external wall tiles of 4 kg/cm² (after 7 days) and a process capability index C_p of 1.0.

Note: 1. Speak with facts and data   2. Make things readily visible using diagrams, charts and lists

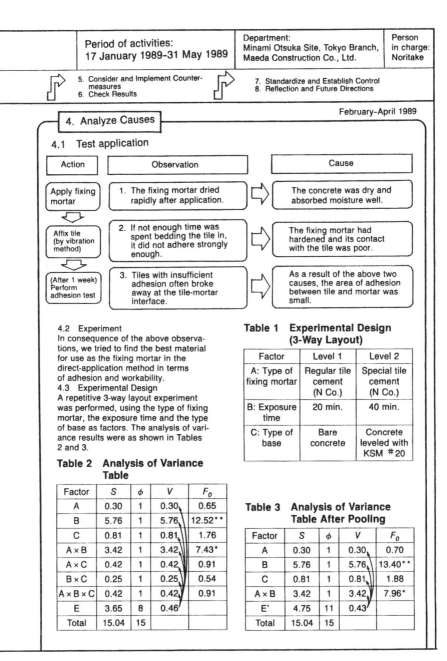

Procedure	1. Reasons for Selecting Topic 3. Set Targets
	2. Understand Situation 4. Analyze Causes

4.4 Summary of Experiments

For the adhesive strength, Factor B (the exposure time) and the interaction A × B were found to be significant, while Factors A and C and the interactions A × C and B × C were nonsignificant. When the population mean and the 95% confidence interval were estimated, the results shown in Figs. 4 and 5 were obtained.

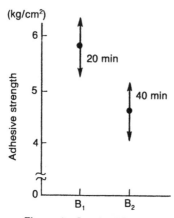

Figure 4   Graph of Significant Factors

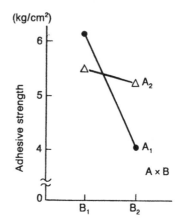

Figure 5   Graph of Significant Factors

The regular tile cement (Factor A) gives the maximum adhesive strength at an exposure time of 20 min, but the adhesive strength drops rapidly when this time is exceeded. In contrast to this, the adhesive strength of the special tile cement is not greatly affected by the exposure time but is lower than the maximum.

5. Consider and Implement Countermeasures   (April 89)

As a result of the above analysis, it was decided at this worksite to use regular tile cement with an exposure time of 20 min or less for the direct application of double-size tiles to external walls. This decision was incorporated into Work Procedure Zne-042r and QC Process Table Zne-043m. The new procedure was taught as a priority quality in the company training program for new trainees.

Note: 1. Speak with facts and data
        2. Make things readily visible using diagrams, charts and lists

Some Examples of the QC Problem-Solving Approach 163

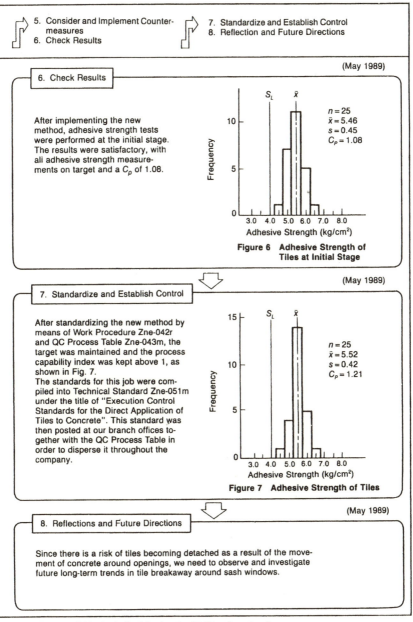

> 5. Consider and Implement Countermeasures
> 6. Check Results
> 7. Standardize and Establish Control
> 8. Reflection and Future Directions

6. Check Results (May 1989)

After implementing the new method, adhesive strength tests were performed at the initial stage. The results were satisfactory, with all adhesive strength measurements on target and a C_p of 1.08.

$n = 25$
$\bar{x} = 5.46$
$s = 0.45$
$C_p = 1.08$

Figure 6 Adhesive Strength of Tiles at Initial Stage

7. Standardize and Establish Control (May 1989)

After standardizing the new method by means of Work Procedure Zne-042r and QC Process Table Zne-043m, the target was maintained and the process capability index was kept above 1, as shown in Fig. 7.
The standards for this job were compiled into Technical Standard Zne-051m under the title of "Execution Control Standards for the Direct Application of Tiles to Concrete". This standard was then posted at our branch offices together with the QC Process Table in order to disperse it throughout the company.

$n = 25$
$\bar{x} = 5.52$
$s = 0.42$
$C_p = 1.21$

Figure 7 Adhesive Strength of Tiles

8. Reflections and Future Directions (May 1989)

Since there is a risk of tiles becoming detached as a result of the movement of concrete around openings, we need to observe and investigate future long-term trends in tile breakaway around sash windows.

3. Report activities logically, following the QC Story format .... keep records based on the 7 Steps

References

Note: all references are in Japanese

1. HOSOTANI, KATSUYA. *QC-teki Mondai Kaiketsuho* (*The QC Problem-Solving Approach*). *Hinshitsu Gekkan Tekisuto* (*QC Text for Quality Month*) 184, Hinshitsu Gekkan Committee, 1987.

2. HOSOTANI, KATSUYA. *QC-teki Mono no Mikata · Kangaekata* (*Japanese Quality Concepts An overview*). JUSE Press Ltd., Tokyo, 1984.

3. JUSE Problem-Solving Research Group, ed. *TQC ni okeru Mondai Kaiketsuho* (*TQC Solution—The 14 Step Process*). JUSE Press Ltd., 1985.

4. HOSOTANI, KATSUYA. *QC Nanatsu Dogu—Yasashii QC Shuho Enshu* (*The Seven QC Tools—A Seminar in Simple QC Methods*). JUSE Press Ltd., 1982.

5. HINO, SHINJI. *Anken Juchu Katsudo ni okeru Urikomi Hoho no Kaizen* (*Improving Sales Techniques in Item Order-Taking*). In *Proceedings of the 9th Seven New QC Tools Symposium*, JUSE Press, Ltd., pp. 139–143, 1987.

6. IGUCHI, MITSUO. *Chogo Mikisa no Funjin Gensho* (*Dust Reduction in Blending Mixer*). In *Proceedings of the 1975th QC Circle Grand Symposium*, QC Circle Kinki Chapter, 1987, pp. 22–24.

7. SYOJI, TOSHIAKI. *PHC Kugiuchi Koji ni okeru Yokyu Hinshitsu no Kakuho to Seko Noritsu no Kojo* (*Securing Required Quality and Improving Work Efficiency in PHC Piledriving*). *Hinshitsu Kanri* (Total Quality Control), 40, (June 1989 spec. ed.): 293–299.

8. ISHIBASHI, NOBUO. *Shin Jidai o Yomikatsu* (*Prophecying the New Era*). Toyo Keizai Shinposha, Tokyo, 1986, pp. 13–17.

9. NISHIZAWA, JUN'ICHI, *Junen Saki o Yomu Hassoho* (*How to Imagine Ten Years Ahead*). Kodansha, Tokyo, 1985, pp. 18–19.

10. The following references (a–j) are all taken from JUSE's *QC Circle* magazine:

    a. MATSUSHITA, MASATO. *Kizuita Koto wa Sugu Tema ni* (*Immediately Take up any Deficiencies Noticed as an Improvement Topic*). 13 (1988): 8–21.

    b. TAKESHITA, MASANORI. *Okyakusama ga Manzoku Suru Kogu Teikyo* (*Providing Tools that Satisfy the Customer*). 13 (1988): 12–15.

c. KOJIMA, SATOSHI, ET AL. *Nyu Maburaito Yokusoo Kettenritsu no Teigen (Reducing the Defect Rate in Artificial Marble Bathtubs).* 320 (1989): 46–51.

d. SUGIYAMA, TETSURO. *Bideo de Furyo Hassei no Mekanizumu o Saigen (Reconstructing Defect Generation Mechanism by VTR).* 322 (1989): 16.

e. SHINOHARA, MITSUYO, ET AL. *Shutcho Shuri Chumonsho Mitchaku 61-nichi Ijo no Teigen (Reducing the 61-Day-and-Over Non-Arrival Rate of On-Site Repair Order Forms).* 319 (1988): 34–39.

f. ISHIBASHI, MITSUYO, ET AL. *Rinji Shohosen no Tenki Ayamari o Herasu (Reduce the Number of Mistakes in Transcribing Emergency Prescription Slips).* 318 (1988): 52–57.

g. SHIMIZU, MASUZO, ET AL. *Tekkinshiki Renzoku Chichuheki Koji ni okeru H-ko Tawamiryo no Teigen (Reducing Drooping of H-Girders in Steel-Reinforced Continuous Underground Wall Construction).* 315 (1988): 34–39.

h. HORIDE, SHIGEOMI, ET AL. *Injekuta Kumitate Chokkoritsu 100% e Chosen (Aiming for a 100% Straight-through Rate in Injector Assembly).* 311 (1988): 40–45.

i. ISHIKAWA, YUKIKO, ET AL. *Taimuriina Shutsuzu o Goryu Sakuru de (Timely Issuing of Drawings by the Confluence Circle).* 321 (1989): 52–57.

j. HOSOTANI, KATSUYA, *Umai Hadome no Shikata (How to Apply the Brakes Skillfully).* 218 (1981): 4–7.

Index

A

Analyze causes 90
"Apply the brakes" 104
Approaches to identifying
problems 76
Auxiliary graphical symbols for process
charts 125

B

Basic graphic symbols for process
charts 124

C

Careless mistakes 25
Check results 102
Classifying problems 14
Companywide quality control 9
Considering and implementing
countermeasures 95
Consumer orientation 28
—three Keys 28
Control characteristics 83
CWQC 9

D

Deming cycle 38, 40
Describe topic 77
—Seven points 77
Dispersion control 55
—key points 55

E

Emergency countermeasures 59
Error-proofing 25
—basic methods 25
Establish control 104

F

Five conditions for well-chosen
topics 79
4-M technique 97
Foolproofing 25
5W1H technique 97

G

Good problem-solvers 5

I

Idea-generating strategies 96
Identifying the facts 48
Individual countermeasures 59
Intangible benefits 102

M

Management by fact 48
"Market in" 26
Minor slips 26

N

Next process 33
—is your customer 33
—7 key points for 34

O

Own process 34

P

PDCA wheel 39
Permanent countermeasures 59
Plan activities 88
Previous process 33
Priority consciousness 43
Priority problems 43

167

INDEX

Problem evaluation chart 78
Problem-solving formula 74
Process control 51
—key points 52
Process symbols 125
"Product out" 26

Q
QC 9
—mindset 21
QC problem-solving approach 17
—definition 18
—process 73
—ten benefits 18
QC Story 137
QC tools 112
—basic procedure for skillful
use 119
—seven key points for 123
—significance of 111
—types of 113
Quality control 9
Quality first 23
—activities 24
—strategies 24

R
Recurrence prevention 59
—countermeasures 59

S
Select topic 75
Seven conditions for well-set
targets 86
Seven hints for skillful
presentations 139
Seven keys to skillful standardization
and control 106
Seven new QC tools 114
Seven QC Tools 113
—overview 116
Seven reasons for preparing
reports 137
Standardization 61, 104
—and establishing control 104
—checkpoints for 66
Standards 61
Statistical methods 113
Strong workplace 7
Systematic countermeasures 60

T
Ten Commandments for workplace
leaders 20
Total quality control 9
TQC 9
—Meaning of 10
—Seven features of 11
TQM 9
Trouble 59

U
Understand situation and set
targets 82
—seven key points 82
Using data 112

W
Waste, unevenness and strain 98
Workplace leaders 1
—role of 2
WUS technique 98